Second Edition

MEDIA MATH

BASIC TECHNIQUES OF MEDIA EVALUATION

Printed on recyclable paper

ROBERT W. HALL

D1157245

NTC Business Books
a division of *NTC Publishing Group* • Lincolnwood, Illinois USA

Library of Congress Cataloging-in-Publication Data

Hall, Robert W. (Robert William)
    Media math : basic techniques of media evaluation / Robert W.
Hall. — 2nd ed.
        p.   cm.
    Includes index.
    ISBN 0-8442-3128-2
    1. Advertising media planning—Mathematics.   I. Title.
    HF5826.5.H35   1991   91-7784
    659.1′01′51—dc20   CIP

1996 Printing

Published by NTC Business Books, a division of NTC Publishing Group
4255 West Touhy Avenue
Lincolnwood (Chicago), Illinois 60646-1975, U.S.A.
    5 6 7 8 9 VP 9 8 7 6 5 4 3

Contents

Introduction

Media Math will provide explanations and examples of mathematical calculations commonly used in the media department of advertising agencies. However, the calculations are not only used in media departments. The principles and processes described in this manual have applications wherever advertising concepts are used, by both the advertiser and the ad agency practitioner.

Every level of advertising uses some math, and if an individual even occasionally uses a calculator, this manual can be helpful. For the media department and the student of advertising, *Media Math* will serve three primary functions:

1. a *checklist* of mathematical processes to be mastered;
2. a *training document* to assure universal exposure to the mathematical concepts and to examples of their applications;
3. a *reference book* for quick review or clarification of mathematical procedures.

The scope of material covered ranges from the most basic utilization of calculators to the complexity of determining broadcast media cost per thousand from cost per gross rating point. All explanations include realistic media examples, and each chapter concludes with unsolved practice problems.

Before you place *Media Math* on a shelf with other reference books, take one of the tests in the back of the manual. Answers to the tests are provided so that individuals can evaluate their skills and see if there are some sections they need to brush up.

1

Calculator Skills

Fundamental to media math is the proper use of a calculator to assure accuracy and speed. There are too many different models of calculators to permit description in this manual. However, each business-level calculator provides the following functions that should be utilized. Ask someone for help if you do not understand how to conduct any of these operations on your calculator.

Decimal Place Selector and Decimal Mode Selector

Let the calculator do the work for you. Permit no more decimal places to show in the answer panel of your calculator than you need. Select the number of decimal places desired and using the *decimal mode selector,* indicate whether the last decimal is to be rounded.

Most media department calculations will be satisfied by setting the decimal selector at 2 or 3 and setting the mode for 5/4 rounding of the last decimal.

5/4 rounding allows the last decimal shown in the calculator answer panel to be increased by one if the next digit has a value of 5 or more, and leaves it unchanged if the next digit is 4 or less. Exception to 5/4 rounding in media calculations is "round-up," used in the preparation of rough data or estimated budgets where it is advantageous for one's data to be on the high side. Round-up always increases the last decimal shown in the answer panel if the next digit is greater than zero. Two other options are often available on a decimal mode selector—the *floating* decimal and the *cut* decimal. Floating allows as many decimal digits as fit in the answer panel. Cut simply cuts off the excess decimal digits without rounding the last digit shown in the answer panel.

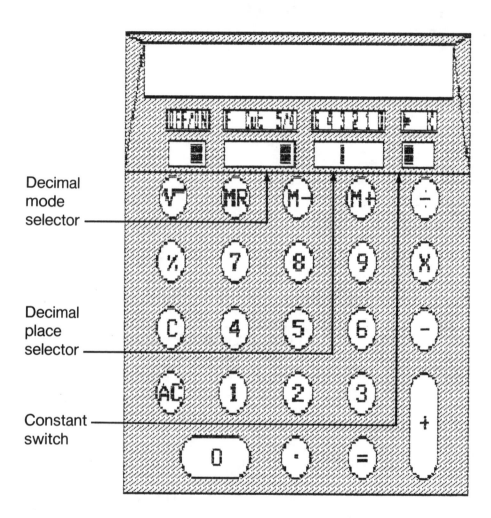

Decimal
mode
selector

Decimal
place
selector

Constant
switch

Numbers displayed in the calculator's answer panel should not be reported any more precisely than the data used in the calculation. For example, the following data does not exceed three decimal places, so the answer generally should not be reported more precisely than three decimal places.

$$0.367 \div 0.074 = 4.9594594$$
$$= 4.959$$

Using a Constant

A series of multiplication or division calculations using the same number (*constant*) can be accomplished more rapidly by using the constant mode of your calculator.

- Most calculators offer the constant mode by a switch marked "K."
- If no K switch is present, the constant may be automatically retained or may require depressing the multiplication/division key twice.
- Once entered, the constant and function (multiplication or division) are retained and repeated. Thereafter, the user need only enter the variable followed by the equal sign. (See examples that follow.)

Multiplication using a constant requires that the first number entered is the constant factor (the number by which all other numbers will be multiplied).

Division by a constant is more complicated if your calculator requires pressing the function key twice. You must first enter the divisor (the number which will be divided into all the other numbers in the series of calculations). See the following examples.

Remember to disengage the K switch when the constant function is not being used. The K setting can interfere with chain calculations.

	Problem	Most Calculators In Media Dept. ("K" Key Set or Built-In Constant)	Pocket Calculators and Some Desk Models (Pressing Function Key Two Times)
Example 1:	**Multiplication**		
	$6 \times 3 = 18$	$3 \times\ \ 6 =$	$3 \times \times\ \ 6 =$
	$9 \times 3 = 27$	$9 =$	$9 =$
	$18 \times 3 = 54$	$18 =$	$18 =$
	$12 \times 3 = 36$	$12 =$	$12 =$
Example 2:	**Division**		
	$6 \div 3 = 2$	$6 \div\ \ 3 =$	$3 \div \div\ \ 6 =$
	$9 \div 3 = 3$	$9 =$	$9 =$
	$18 \div 3 = 6$	$18 =$	$18 =$
	$12 \div 3 = 4$	$12 =$	$12 =$

Problem	Most Calculators In Media Dept. ("K" Key Set or Built-In Constant)	Pocket Calculators and Some Desk Models (Pressing Function Key Two Times)
Example 3: **Multiplication**		
$4 \times 2 = 8$	$4 \times 2 =$	$4 \times \times 2 =$
$4 \times 4 = 16$	$4 =$	$4 =$
$4 \times 8 = 16$	$8 =$	$8 =$
$4 \times 3 = 12$	$3 =$	$3 =$
$4 \times 10 = 40$	$10 =$	$10 =$
Example 4: **Division**		
$8.0 \div 4 = 2$	$8 \div 4 =$	$4 \div \div 8 =$
$12.0 \div 4 = 3$	$12 =$	$12 =$
$160.0 \div 4 = 40$	$160 =$	$160 =$
$93.6 \div 4 = 23.4$	$93.6 =$	$93.6 =$
$474.0 \div 4 = 118.5$	$474 =$	$474 =$

Calculator Logic

Just as calculators have different ways of handling constants, they also have two distinct methods for data input. Before giving more explanations and calculations, it is necessary to distinguish between these two *logic systems* common to calculators. The logic system dictates the procedure you must follow for entering numbers into your calculator.

Arithmetic Logic is typical of business-grade calculators. The calculators usually have an equal sign sharing space with the plus and minus signs ($+ =$, and $- =$). Each number entered must be followed by a function key ($+, -, \times, \div$) that applies to *that* number. The final entry of multiplication or division must be followed by an equal sign ($+ =$) or a percent sign (%). The input procedure of arithmetic logic cannot be ignored if time–saving chain calculations are to be utilized. (Chain calculations are the next topic in this chapter.)

The calculation of 7 plus 2 would be entered

$$7 + =$$
$$2 + =$$

The calculation of 7 minus 2 would be entered

$$7 + =$$
$$2 - =$$

4

Note: The following entry is a common error that results in a negative answer. It will also distort chain calculations.

$$7 - =$$
$$2 + =$$

The calculation of 12 times 3 would be entered

$$12 \times$$
$$3 + =$$

The calculation of 9 divided by 3 would be entered

$$9 \div$$
$$3 + =$$

Algebraic Logic is typical of pocket and home calculators. The calculators have a key dedicated exclusively to the equal sign (=). Each number entered is followed by a function key (+, −, ×, ÷) that applies to the *next* number and concludes with an equal sign (=) or a percent sign (%).

The calculation of 7 plus 2 would be entered

$$7 +$$
$$2 =$$

The calculation of 7 minus 2 would be entered

$$7 -$$
$$2 =$$

The calculation of 12 times 3 would be entered

$$12 \times$$
$$3 =$$

The calculation of 9 divided by 3 would be entered

$$9 \div$$
$$3 =$$

Chain Calculations

Sequences of calculations, where each step utilizes the answer from the previous step, are common in media. Most calculators permit acceleration of these calculations by eliminating interim equal signs (=) between the first and final steps of calculation.

The following examples of chain calculations provide the keys and sequence of both types of mathematical logic.

Problem	Most Calculators in Media Department (Arithmetic Logic)	Pocket Calculators and Some Desk Models (Algebraic Logic)

Example 1: $[(9 + 7 - 4) \div 3] \times 6 = 24$

	9 + =	9 +
	7 + =	7 −
	4 − =	4 ÷
	÷	3 ×
	3 ×	6 =
	6 + =	

Note that it is unnecessary to enter an equal sign between the division and multiplication chain of calculations.

Example 2: $[(21 \div 7) \times 6] + 15 = 33$

	21 ÷	21 ÷
	7 ×	7 ×
	6 + =	6 +
	15 + =	15 =

Example 3: $[(15 \times 3) \div 5] - 4 = 5$

	15 ×	15 ×
	3 ÷	3 ÷
	5 + =	5 −
	4 − =	4 =

Example 4: $[(4 \times 7) \div 2] + 3 = 17$

	4 ×	4 ×
	7 ÷	7 ÷
	2 + =	2 +
	3 + =	3 =

Example 5: Add the sales of the last three months, divide the sum by 3, then multiply by 12.

$[(\$525,000 + \$515,000 + \$610,000) \div 3] \times 12 = \$6,600,000$

	525,000 + =	525,000 +
	515,000 + =	515,000 +
	610,000 + =	610,000 ÷
	÷	3 ×
	3 ×	12 =
	12 + =	

Example 6:   In the last three rating books, Program A had audiences of 125,000, 113,000, and 122,000. Combine the three audience figures, divide by 3, and multiply the answer by 0.9.

$$[(125,000 + 113,000 + 122,000) \div 3] \times 0.9 = 108,000$$

125,000 + =	125,000 +
113,000 + =	113,000 +
122,000 + =	122,000 ÷
÷	3 ×
3 ×	.9 =
.9 + =	

Memory Calculations   The memory capacity of your calculator permits the accumulation of data from many independent calculations. It can save significant time that would otherwise be spent re-entering answers from contributing calculations.

Although the procedures for utilizing the memory functions differ among calculators, most use a four key system.

> M+: Add to memory
> M−: Subtract from memory
> RM: Read memory
> CM: Clear memory

Applications of the memory are varied and limitless. Note that the solution to each individual calculation is shown in the calculator's display panel and can be copied sequentially onto a worksheet.

Hit the clear memory (CM) key of the calculator before beginning each new problem using memory.

Be aware that in the following examples some calculators may require an equal sign (=) prior to M+ or M− key entry in order to solve component calculations.

Problem	Most Calculators In Media Dept. (Arithmetic Logic)	Pocket Calculators and Some Desk Models (Algebraic Logic)
Example 1:	CM	CM
6 × 7 = 42	6 × 7 M+	6 × 7 M+
4 × 5 = 20	4 × 5 M+	4 × 5 M+
2 × 19 = 38	2 × 19 M+	2 × 19 M+
3 × 12 = 36	3 × 12 M+	3 × 12 M+
10 × 14 = 140	10 × 14 M+	10 × 14 M+
5 × 15 = 75	5 × 15 M+	5 × 15 M+
Total 351	RM	RM
351 ÷ 6 = 58.5	÷ 6 + =	÷ 6 =

		CM	CM
Example 2:			
$84 \div 4 = 21$		$84 \div 4$ M+	$84 \div 4$ M+
$160 \div 5 = 32$		$160 \div 5$ M+	$160 \div 5$ M+
$36 \div 6 = 6$		$36 \div 6$ M+	$36 \div 6$ M+
$440 \div 11 = 40$		$440 \div 11$ M+	$440 \div 11$ M+
$840 \div 8 = \underline{105}$		$840 \div 8$ M+	$840 \div 8$ M+
Total	$\overline{204}$	RM	RM
$204 \times 4 = 816$		$\times 4 + =$	$\times 4 =$

		Set Constant; CM	CM
Example 3:			
$21 \div 7 = 3$		$21 \div 7$ M+	$7 \div \div 21$ M+
$35 \div 7 = 5$		35 M+	35 M+
$28 \div 7 = 4$		28 M+	28 M+
$56 \div 7 = 8$		56 M+	56 M+
$105 \div 7 = \underline{15}$		105 M+	105 M+
Total	$\overline{35}$	RM	RM
$35 \times 1.4 = 49$		$\times 1.4 + =$	$\times 1.4 =$

		Set Constant; CM	CM
Example 4:			
$47 \times 5 = 235$		5×47 M+	$5 \times \times 47$ M+
$39 \times 5 = 195$		39 M+	39 M+
$45 \times 5 = 225$		45 M+	45 M+
$53 \times 5 = \underline{265}$		53 M+	53 M+
Total	$\overline{920}$	RM	RM
Subtract:			
$(27 \times 5 = 135)$		27 M−	27 M−
$(37 \times 5 = \underline{185})$		37 M−	37 M−
Total	$\overline{600}$	RM	RM

Miscellaneous Functions

Many media department calculators have additional functions that will be helpful. Be sure to explore and utilize the full potential of your machine. Some helpful functions to have include the following:

Item Count
Sign Change
Register Change
Delta Percent
Automatic Add of Two Decimals
Second Memory
Right-Shift Key for Digit Deletion

Chapter 1 Review Problems

Set the calculator decimal place selector at 3. Set the decimal mode selector at 5/4. Solve the following problems.

1. Addition

A.
```
      521.0
       31.07
       54.1
      147.369
        8.632
  + 1,009.4
```

B.
```
        6
       12
      132
       67
       91
   + 403
```

C.
```
       61.0000
       45.3701
       93.0123
      106.7082
   +    9.1520
```

D.
```
       19.0004
       56.0372
       14.3521
       61.0843
   + 75.6792
```

2. Subtraction

A.
```
    23.04
  -  9.075
```

B.
```
    390.0009
  - 288.0003
```

C.
```
    167.1234
  -  39.9876
  -  15.0098
  -  72.8463
```

D.
```
    191.31
  -   4.023
  -  16.571
  -  31.403
```

3. Multiplication

A.   27
   ×36

B.   14.791
   × 3.54

C.   49.1
   × 6.937

D.   92.0437
   ×127.2

4. Division

A. $326.9 \div 16 =$ _____

B. $664.9 \div 41.7 =$ _____

C. $31.9157 \div 0.58 =$ _____

D. $1{,}897.2 \div 6.192 =$ _____

5. Using a constant

A. $6 \times 9 =$ _____
  $15 \times 9 =$ _____
  $12 \times 9 =$ _____
  $47 \times 9 =$ _____

B. $23 \div 12 =$ _____
  $14 \div 12 =$ _____
  $80 \div 12 =$ _____
  $38 \div 12 =$ _____

C. $9.7 \times 61 \ =$ _____
  $9.7 \times 3 \ =$ _____
  $9.7 \times 8.3 =$ _____
  $9.7 \times 36.1 =$ _____
  $9.7 \times 0.5 =$ _____

D. $16.9 \times 5.61 =$ _____
  $16.9 \times 41.02 =$ _____
  $16.9 \times 0.87 =$ _____
  $4.2 \times 16.9 \ =$ _____
  $51 \ \times 16.9 \ =$ _____

E. $103 \div 2.7 = \rule{2cm}{0.4pt}$ F. $\$1,841 \div 52 = \rule{2cm}{0.4pt}$
 $97.6 \div 2.7 = \rule{2cm}{0.4pt}$ $\$4,658 \div 52 = \rule{2cm}{0.4pt}$
 $19.9 \div 2.7 = \rule{2cm}{0.4pt}$ $\$3,217 \div 52 = \rule{2cm}{0.4pt}$
 $83 \div 2.7 = \rule{2cm}{0.4pt}$ $\$8,102 \div 52 = \rule{2cm}{0.4pt}$

6. Chain calculations

 A. $9 + 7 + 12 + 14 + 15 - 5 - 21 = \rule{3cm}{0.4pt}$

 B. $(5 \times 4) + 15 + 6 - 9 = \rule{3cm}{0.4pt}$

 C. $[(51.5 \times 31.2) \div 5.7] + 1.9 + 2.1 = \rule{3cm}{0.4pt}$

 D. $[(\$425 + \$791 + \$873) \div 3] \times 0.94 = \rule{3cm}{0.4pt}$

 E. $[(\$921 \div 7) \times 15] + \$248 + \$327 = \rule{3cm}{0.4pt}$

7. Memory calculations

 A. $7 \times 5 =$
  $12 \times 5 =$
  $206 \times 5 =$
  $149 \times 5 =$
  $61 \times 5 = \rule{1.5cm}{0.4pt}$

  Total $\rule{1.5cm}{0.4pt} \div 3 = \rule{1.5cm}{0.4pt}$

 B. $73.6 \times 4.1 =$
  $84.7 \times 12.3 =$
  $65.0 \times 15.7 =$
  $41.2 \times 9.9 = \rule{1.5cm}{0.4pt}$

  Total $\rule{1.5cm}{0.4pt} \times 12 = \rule{1.5cm}{0.4pt}$

 C. $\$571,431 \div 12 =$
  $\$395,789 \div 12 =$
  $\$378,989 \div 12 =$
  $\$608,365 \div 12 =$
  $\$431,706 \div 12 = \rule{1.5cm}{0.4pt}$

  Total $\rule{1.5cm}{0.4pt} \div 5 = \rule{1.5cm}{0.4pt}$

D. 627.01 ÷ 9 =
97.291 ÷ 2 =
957.607 ÷ 11 =
534.9 ÷ 6 = _____
Sub-Total

Subtract   75.673

Total   _____

E. 89.6 × 5 =
93 ÷ 3 =
41.2 × 9 =
176.8 ÷ 8 =
15.1 × 9 = _____

Total   _____

2 Percentages

Percentages express a numerical relationship in hundredths (1/100 or 0.01). Percent means hundredths and is symbolized by the symbol "%." Percentages may be expressed as a common fraction or as a decimal.

For example:

$$2\% = \frac{2}{100}* \quad \text{and} \quad .02$$

$$30\% = \frac{30}{100}* \quad \text{and} \quad .30$$

$$75\% = \frac{75}{100}* \quad \text{and} \quad .75$$

$$125\% = \frac{125}{100}* \quad \text{and} \quad 1.25$$

*The fractions above can be further reduced, for example,

$$\frac{2}{100} = \frac{1}{50} \qquad \frac{30}{100} = \frac{3}{10}$$

$$\frac{75}{100} = \frac{3}{4} \qquad \frac{125}{100} = 1\frac{1}{4}$$

Changing Percents to Decimals

To change a percent to a decimal, drop the % symbol and write in a decimal point two places to the left. Here are eight examples.

$$
\begin{array}{ll}
4\% = .04 & 6.4\% = .064 \\
25\% = .25 & 37.5\% = .375 \\
80\% = .80 & 91.6\% = .916 \\
265\% = 2.65 & 419.7\% = 4.197
\end{array}
$$

Changing Decimals to Percents

To change decimals to percents, move the decimal point two places to the right and attach the % symbol. Following are eight examples.

$$
\begin{array}{rll}
.07 \ (& 7 \ \text{hundredths}) = & 7\% \\
.63 \ (& 63 \ \text{hundredths}) = & 63\% \\
1.52 \ (& 152 \ \text{hundredths}) = & 152\% \\
39.21 \ (3{,}921 \ \text{hundredths}) = & 3{,}921\% \\
.004 \ (& 0.4 \ \text{hundredths}) = & 0.4\% \\
.092 \ (& 9.2 \ \text{hundredths}) = & 9.2\% \\
.625 \ (& 62.5 \ \text{hundredths}) = & 62.5\% \\
2.543 \ (& 254.3 \ \text{hundredths}) = & 254.3\%
\end{array}
$$

Changing Common Fractions to Percents

To change fractions to percents requires two steps. *First,* divide the numerator (top number) by the denominator (bottom number) to get a decimal.

Second, move the decimal point two places to the right and attach the % symbol. Following are eight examples.

$$
\begin{array}{lllll}
1/4 = & 1 \div 4 = & .25 \ (& 25 \ \text{hundredths}) = & 25\% \\
3/5 = & 3 \div 5 = & .60 \ (& 60 \ \text{hundredths}) = & 60\% \\
3/4 = & 3 \div 4 = & .75 \ (& 75 \ \text{hundredths}) = & 75\% \\
24/32 = & 24 \div 32 = & .75 \ (& 75 \ \text{hundredths}) = & 75\% \\
12/15 = & 12 \div 15 = & .80 \ (& 80 \ \text{hundredths}) = & 80\% \\
7/4 = & 7 \div 4 = & 1.75 \ (175 \ \text{hundredths}) = & 175\% \\
12/32 = & 12 \div 32 = & .375 \ (37.5 \ \text{hundredths}) = & 37.5\% \\
5/8 = & 5 \div 8 = & .625 \ (62.5 \ \text{hundredths}) = & 62.5\%
\end{array}
$$

Using your calculator makes converting fractions to percents even easier. Divide the numerator by the denominator but press the % key instead of the equals (=) key. The decimal point is properly repositioned for you, and you need only attach the % symbol. Here are eight calculator examples.

Calculator setting: Two–decimal selection, 5/4 rounding of last digit.

$$
\begin{aligned}
1/2 &= 1 \div 2 \quad \% \quad \text{answer} \quad 50\% \\
27/36 &= 27 \div 36 \quad \% \quad \text{answer} \quad 75\% \\
4/5 &= 4 \div 5 \quad \% \quad \text{answer} \quad 80\% \\
48/60 &= 48 \div 60 \quad \% \quad \text{answer} \quad 80\% \\
2/3 &= 2 \div 3 \quad \% \quad \text{answer} \quad 66.67\% \\
5/6 &= 5 \div 6 \quad \% \quad \text{answer} \quad 83.33\% \\
54/34 &= 54 \div 34 \quad \% \quad \text{answer} \quad 158.82\% \\
7/3 &= 7 \div 3 \quad \% \quad \text{answer} \quad 233.33\%
\end{aligned}
$$

Finding a Percent of a Number

Suppose you are asked what is 4% of 50. This means you want to find 4 hundredths of 50.

Note: In mathematics, "of" means "times" (multiplication).

"4% of 50" means 4% times 50.

Similarly, "is" means "equals."

"What *is* 4% *of* 50?"   means   ? = 4% × 50

To find the percent of a number, without using a calculator, first change the percent to a decimal;

4% becomes .04

then multiply that decimal times the number.

.04 × 50 = 2.00 or 2

If you use a calculator, the procedure is even easier. Enter the percentage times the number, then press %.

4 × 50   %   The answer is 2.

Note: In multiplication, it does not make any difference as to the order in which numbers are multiplied.

$$
\begin{aligned}
4\% \times 50 &= 50 \times 4\% \\
.04 \times 50 &= 50 \times .04 \\
2 \times 3 \times 6 = 2 \times 6 \times 3 &= 3 \times 2 \times 6 = 3 \times 6 \times 2 = \\
6 \times 2 \times 3 &= 6 \times 3 \times 2
\end{aligned}
$$

Here are some more examples for use on your calculator: Calculator setting: Two–decimal selection, 5/4 rounding of last digit.

Find 30% of 72 =	30 × 72	%	answer	21.6
Find 67% of 915 =	67 × 915	%	answer	613.05
Find 12.5% of 64 =	12.5 × 64	%	answer	8
Find 250% of 32 =	250 × 32	%	answer	80
What number is 15% of 210?	15 × 210	%	answer	31.5
What number is 40% of 60?	40 × 60	%	answer	24
What number is 22.3% of 93?	22.3 × 93	%	answer	20.74
What number is 160% of 56?	160 × 56	%	answer	89.6
Take 80% of 27 =	80 × 27	%	answer	21.6
Take 15% of $579 =	15 × 579	%	answer	$86.85

Finding What Percent One Number Is of Another Number

Look at the statement 20% of 80 = 16. Principles of mathematics permit us to change the order of the equation to 20% = 16 ÷ 80 (by dividing each side of the equation by 80). Now suppose we were asked, "16 is what percent of 80?" The formula shows us that we can divide 16 by 80 to determine the percentage.

Following are some exercises in finding percentages. Use your calculator and check your answers against the answers provided. If you have trouble remembering which number to divide by, write the formula, then solve the problem.

Calculator setting: Two–decimal selection, 5/4 rounding of last digit.

Problem	Formula	Calculator	Answer
8 is what % of 15?	8 = ?% × 15		
	8 ÷ 15 = ?%	8 ÷ 15 %	53.33%
45 is what % of 72?	45 = ?% × 72		
	45 ÷ 72 = ?%	45 ÷ 72 %	62.5%
30 is what % of 360?	30 = ?% × 360		
	30 ÷ 350 = ?%	30 ÷ 360 %	8.33%
75 is what % of 50?	75 = ?% × 50		
	75 ÷ 50 = ?%	75 ÷ 50 %	150%
15 is what % of 90?	15 = ?% × 90		
	15 ÷ 90 = ?%	15 ÷ 90 %	16.67%

Problem	Formula	Calculator	Answer
1.5 is what % of 9?	1.5 = ?% × 9 1.5 ÷ 9 = ?%	1.5 ÷ 9 %	16.67%
275 is what % of 400?	275 = ?% × 400 275 ÷ 400 = ?%	275 ÷ 400 %	68.75%
0.9 is what % of 3.6?	0.9 = ?% × 3.6 0.9 ÷ 3.6 = ?%	0.9 ÷ 3.6 %	25%
90 is what % of 360?	90 = ?% × 360 90 ÷ 360 = ?%	90 ÷ 360 %	25%
9 is what % of 360?	9 = ?% × 360 9 ÷ 360 = ?%	9 ÷ 360 %	2.5%

Finding Percent Using a Constant

When more than one number is percentaged against the same number, the calculations can be accelerated by using the "constant" function of your calculator. (Review "Using a Constant" in chapter 1, and follow the examples below.)

Example 1:

Express each medium's cost as a percent of the total advertising budget.

	Expenditure (000)
Magazines	$1,765
Television	9,884
Newspapers	3,883
Outdoor	2,118
Total	$17,650

	"K" key or Built-in Constant			Using ÷ Key Twice		
Magazines	1765 ÷ 17650	%	10%	17650 ÷ ÷ 1765	%	10%
Television	9884	%	56%	9884	%	56%
Newspapers	3883	%	22%	3883	%	22%
Outdoor	2118	%	12%	2118	%	12%
Total			100%			100%

Note: If you press the memory key (M+) instead of %, the memory will accumulate the total of all percentages as a decimal and memory recall (MR or RM) will show the total which should equal 1.00 (decimal equivalent of 100%) and provide a check of your answer.

Example 2: Express each of the following program's audience as a percent of total viewing.

Calculator setting: Two–decimal selection, 5/4 rounding of last digit. Use constant and memory.

	Audience
Program A	20,110
Program B	13,830
Program C	16,170
Program D	7,430
All Other	5,980
Total	63,520

	"K" key or Built-in Constant		Using ÷ Key Twice	
Program A	20110 ÷ 63520 M+	32%	63520 ÷ ÷ 20110 M+	32%
Program B	13830 M+	22%	13830 M+	22%
Program C	16170 M+	25%	16170 M+	25%
Program D	7430 M+	12%	7430 M+	12%
All Other	5980 M+	9%	5980 M+	9%
Total	MR	100%	MR	100%

Finding a Number When a Percent Is Known

Suppose you are told that 6 is 25% of an unknown number, and you want to find that number. Those comfortable with math will tell you that the number is 24. They multiplied 6 × 4 or 6 ÷ 25%, but that is not easy logic for many people. If you have trouble, follow these instructions:

1. Write down the problem as a formula.

   $6 = 25\% \times n$

2. Divide both sides by the % so that n stands alone.

$$\frac{6}{25\%} = \frac{25\% \times n}{25\%} \qquad \frac{6}{25/100} = \frac{(25/100) \times n}{25/100}$$

$$24 = (1) \times n \qquad \frac{6}{1/4} = \frac{(1/4) \times n}{1/4}$$

$$24 = n \qquad 24 = n$$

Here are four examples to solve.
Calculator entries are shown in parentheses.

Example 1:

85% of a magazine's space cost is $100. Find the total cost of the magazine space.

$$85\% \times \text{cost} = \$100$$
$$\text{cost} = \$100 \div 85\% \quad (100 \div 85 \ \%)$$
$$\text{cost} = \$117.65$$

Example 2:

17 is 40% of what number?

$$17 = 40\% \times n$$
$$17 \div 40\% = n \qquad (17 \div 40 \ \%)$$
$$42.5 = n$$

Example 3:

46 is 115% of what number?

$$46 = 115\% \times n$$
$$46 \div 115\% = n \qquad (46 \div 115 \ \%)$$
$$40 = n$$

Example 4:

An ad agency received $6,225 in commission on a magazine space order. The commission was 15% of the space cost. What was the full cost of the magazine ad?

$$\$6,225 = 15\% \times n$$
$$6,225 \div 15\% = n \qquad (6225 \div 15 \ \%)$$

Comparing and Combining Percentages

Percentages can be compared and even combined provided they have a common base—provided they are percentages of the same number or value.

For example, in the illustration below, we can compare and combine the percentages because they have a common base—the percent of United States TV households:

Television Territories	% of U.S. TV Households
Northeast	22%
East Central	15%
West Central	17%
South	29%
Pacific (Plus Alaska & Hawaii)	17%
Total U.S.	100%

- The Pacific plus the Northeast territories total 39% of United States TV households (17% + 22%).

- The South is larger than the Pacific territory. It is larger by 12% in terms of United States TV households (29% − 17%; also expressed as "12 points larger").

- The Northeast is about one and a half times the size of the East Central territory in terms of TV households (22% ÷ 15% = 1.47).

- The West Central and Pacific territories are of equal size in terms of the number of TV households (17% = 17%).

Percentages with differing bases, such as the cable penetration figures below, cannot legitimately or meaningfully be combined because they are not directly related.

Television Territories	% of U.S. TV Households	Cable TV Penetration, Cable connected TV HH as % of Territory TV Households
Northeast	22%	34%
East Central	15%	36%
West Central	17%	27%
South	29%	36%
Pacific (Plus AK & HI)	17%	33%
Total U.S.	100%	33%

- Although the East Central and South Territories each have 36% cable TV penetration, they represent a significantly different number of households. The East Central cable households are 36% of 15% of United States TV households or 5% of the United States. The South has 36% of 29% of United States TV households or 10% of the United States.

- Note that by applying the cable penetration percentage to the TV household % of the United States, we converted the values to a common base that can be compared. The East Central cable penetration is equal to 5% of United States TV households (36% × 15%). In contrast, the South cable penetration is equal to 10% of United States TV households (36% × 29%). The number of homes in the South receiving cable is twice as large as the number of the cable homes in the East Central territory (10% ÷ 5% = 2 or twice as large).

Chapter 2 Review Problems

1. Change the following percents to decimals.

A.   5% =_____   F.   3.8 % =_____

B.   17% =_____   G.   1.36% =_____

C.   63% =_____   H.   21.3 % =_____

D. 142% =_____   I.   297.61% =_____

E. 1,371% =_____   J. 4,002.5 % =_____

2. Change the following decimals to percents.

A.   .06 =_____   F.   .032 =_____

B.   .12 =_____   G.   .271 =_____

C. 3.91 =_____   H. 1.009 =_____

D. 22.47 =_____   I. 47.123 =_____

E.   .004 =_____   J.   4   =_____

3. Using your calculator, change the following fractions to percents.

   Set the calculator's decimal place selector at 2. Set the decimal mode selector at 5/4.

A.   3/5 =_____   F.   9/15 =_____

B.   7/8 =_____   G. 21/33 =_____

C.   7/16 =_____   H. 40/60 =_____

D.   1/32 =_____   I.   15/7 =_____

E. 192/64 =_____   J. 365/550 =_____

4. Using your calculator, complete the following exercises in figuring percents.

   Set the calculator's decimal place selector at 2. Set the decimal mode selector at 5/4.

   A. Find 40% of 38 = _____

   B. Find 38% of $40 = _____

   C. Find 8% of 365 = _____

   D. Find 125% of 52 = _____

   E. Take 67% of 149 = _____

   F. Take 0.9% of $86 = _____

   G. What is 12% of 94? _____

   H. What is 60% of 72? _____

   I. What is 4% of 981? _____

   J. What is 85% of $41,372? _____

5. Determine the missing percentages using your calculator.

   Set the calculator decimal place selector at 2. Set the decimal mode selector at 5/4.

   A.   3 is what % of 12? _____

   B.   27 is what % of 81? _____

   C.   83 is what % of 120? _____

   D. 301 is what % of 508? _____

   E.   5.1 is what % of 35.7? _____

F. 0.6 is what % of 4.2? _____

G. $14 is what % of $45? _____

H. 35 is what % of 7? _____

I. 3.5 is what % of 7? _____

J. $86 is what % of $1,492? _____

6. Find the total and then, using the constant function of your calculator, determine the percentages each element is of the total. Accumulate the total of the percentages without re-entry of the data by utilizing the memory function of your calculator. Use a three-decimal setting with 5/4 rounding of the last digit.

A.

Network News	Audience (000)	3 Net Share (%)
Net A	10,480	
Net B	12,650	
Net C	10,390	_____
Total		

B.

Month	Sales	Percent of Total
January	$207,361	
February	285,170	
March	314,783	
April	469,821	
May	456,905	

Month	Sales	Percent of Total
June	323,074	
July	210,432	
August	193,092	
September	196,611	
October	241,540	
November	342,928	
December	418,096	_____
Total		

C. Advertising	Expenditures	Percent of Total
1st. Quarter	$1,250,300	
2nd. Quarter	1,420,800	
3rd. Quarter	912,200	
4th. Quarter	2,375,600	_____
Total		

7. Solve the following problems, given the percentage. Use a two-decimal setting with 5/4 rounding of the last digit.

A.   60 is   35% of what number?_____

B.   35 is   5% of what number?_____

C.   180 is   20% of what number?_____

D.   76 is 150% of what number?_____

E. 5,872 is   80% of what number?_____

F.   19 is 3.8% of what number?_____

G. 148.2 is 24.7% of what number?_____

H.   61.5 is 0.75% of what number?_____

I. 85% of a newspaper's advertising page cost is $22,355. Find the total cost of the newspaper space.

J. An ad agency received 15% of the total cost of a radio schedule. If the agency received $352,500, how much was the total cost of the radio schedule?

8. After converting the given percentages to a common base, determine the percentage of male viewers for all four programs. *Hint:* Use the % key and the memory function (M+) to accumulate the number of male viewers, then divide the total number of male viewers by the total number of adult viewers. Round male viewers to the nearest thousand and the percentage to a whole percent by setting the decimal at "0" with a 5/4 rounding of the last digit on your calculator.

Program	No. of Adult Viewers (000)	% of Program that are Male Viewers
Program A	44,062	52%
Program B	6,998	83%
Program C	11,079	44%
Program D	31,128	58%
Total	93,267	

3

Agency Commission

Most media provide a 15% commission on space and time charges to accredited advertising agencies. The media cost aside from the agency commission is called the *net* cost and is equal to 85% of the total cost. The total cost including the commission is called the *gross* cost.

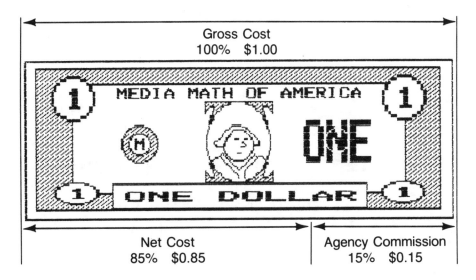

| Gross Cost |
| 100% $1.00 |

MEDIA MATH OF AMERICA — ONE — ONE DOLLAR

| Net Cost | Agency Commission |
| 85% $0.85 | 15% $0.15 |

Agency commission	= 15% of the gross cost.
Net cost	= 85% of the gross cost or gross cost minus the agency commission.
Gross cost	= net cost ÷ agency commission or net cost ÷ 85%.

Advertising agency compensation may be based on a commission or on a fee, depending on the agency-client agreement. The media department is often expected to breakout the commission when reporting media expenditures.

In its simplest form, the system works as follows:

- The client pays the total media cost (gross cost) to the agency.

- The agency pays the net cost to the advertising vehicles (the media).

- The agency retains the commission, and if on a fee basis, credits the commission towards the fee.

Agency commission calculations are simply applications of percentages. Following are examples in agency commission. Calculator entries are shown in parentheses.

Example 1:   Magazine A has a gross space rate of $40,000. Determine the net space cost and agency commission.

$$\text{Net cost} = 85\% \text{ of gross cost}$$
$$= 85\% \times \$40,000 \qquad (85 \times 40000 \; \%)$$
$$= \$34,000$$

$$\text{Agency commission} = 15\% \text{ of gross cost}$$
$$= 15\% \times \$40,000 \qquad (15 \times 40000 \; \%)$$
$$= \$6,000$$

Example 2:   An agency purchased $12 million gross worth of television time for its client. What is the agency commission?

$$\text{Agency commission} = 15\% \text{ of gross cost}$$
$$= 15\% \times \$12,000,000 \quad (15 \times 12000000 \; \%)$$
$$= \$1,800,000$$

Example 3:   A local newspaper charges $1,275 per page. It does not allow agency commission. In order to receive 15% commission, what gross cost must the agency charge its client?

$$\text{Gross cost} = \text{net cost} \div 85\%$$
$$= \$1,275 \div 85\% \qquad (1275 \div 85 \; \%)$$
$$= \$1,500$$

Note: Dividing by 85% is mathematically the same as multiplying by 1.1765 (because $1/.85 = 1.1765$). Therefore, net cost $\times$ 1.1765 = gross cost.

Most media calculations of gross cost from a given net cost are based on multiplying the net by 1.1765; so it is a good number to memorize. When using this multiplication factor, round to the nearest whole dollar.

Example 4:

The cost of a full–page ad in the local college football program is $600. Since the college does not allow agency commission, what would the gross cost be to the client if the agency took commission? Round to the nearest dollar.

Gross cost = net cost $\times$ 1.1765
= $600 $\times$ 1.1765   (600 $\times$ 1.1765 =)
= $706

Chapter 3 Review Problems

Find the missing values.

Round to the nearest dollar.

	Gross Cost	Net Cost	Agency Commission
A.	100%	_____%	15%
B.	$ 1,000	$ 850	$ _____
C.	$ 53,420	$ _____	$ 8,013
D.	$ _____	$ 107,100	$ 18,900
E.	$ _____	$ 26,742	$ 4,719
F.	$ 359,600	$ _____	$ _____
G.	$ 562,750	$ _____	$ _____
H.	$ _____	$ 500,000	$ _____
I.	$ _____	$ 150,000	$ _____
J.	$ _____	$ 40,000	$ _____

4 Indexing

This process allows us to express a number or a group of numbers in relation to one specific number (the *base*). In reality, an index number is nothing more than a percentage of the base number, without the percentage sign (%).

Indexing is a simple two-step process.

1. Select the base, that is, the number you want all other numbers compared to.

2. Divide all the other numbers by the base after dividing the base by 100.
   - For simplicity, just move the decimal place of the base number two places to the left, then divide it into all the numbers.
   - Express the index as a whole number (no decimals).

The process results in the base always having an index of 100.

Using the constant function of your calculator, follow along with the examples. Set the decimal place selector at 0, with 5/4 rounding of the last digit.

Example 1: With 1982 as the base year, index Brand X sales for each year are shown below.

Year	Sales ($000)
1980	3,752
1981	3,865
1982 (base)	3,942
1983	4,178
1984	4,387
1985	4,607

Answer:

Procedure: Divide all sales values by 39.42 (base $\div$ 100).

Year	Sales ($000)	Index
1980	3,752	95
1981	3,865	98
1982 (base)	3,942	100
1983	4,178	106
1984	4,387	111
1985	4,607	117

Interpretation: 1983 sales are 6% greater (106) than 1982 sales; 1985 sales are 17% ahead of those for 1982; 1980 sales are only 95% of 1982's, or 5% below the sales of the base year.

Example 2: Using the data in example 1, re-index the sales making 1980 the base year.

Year	Sales ($000)
1980 (base)	3,752
1981	3,865
1982	3,942
1983	4,178
1984	4,387
1985	4,607

Answer:

Procedure: Divide all sales values by 37.52 (base ÷ 100).

Year	Sales ($000)	Index
1980 (base)	3,752	100
1981	3,865	103
1982	3,942	105
1983	4,178	111
1984	4,387	117
1985	4,607	123

Interpretation: 1983 sales are 11% greater (111) than 1980 sales; 1985 sales are 23% ahead of 1980's. 1983, 1984, and 1985 sales each showed a consistent six-point gain in the index compared to the previous year.

Example 3:

Brand X's advertising spending for the average month is $920,000. Index each month's spending to the average.

January	$ 300,000	July	$ 654,000
February	988,000	August	700,000
March	1,140,000	September	900,000
April	1,150,000	October	963,000
May	940,000	November	1,200,000
June	680,000	December	1,425,000

Answer:

Procedure: Divide each month's spending by $9,200 (base ÷ 100).

Month	Spending	Index
January	$ 300,000	33
February	988,000	107
March	1,140,000	124
April	1,150,000	125
May	940,000	102
June	680,000	74
July	654,000	71

Month	Spending	Index
August	700,000	76
September	900,000	98
October	963,000	105
November	1,200,000	130
December	1,425,000	155

Interpretation: March, April, November, and December are substantially above average spending months, with December 55% above the average. January is the lowest month of spending—only 33% of the average month.

Example 4: Using the data in example 3, re-index the spending to the month of May.

January	$ 300,000	July	$ 654,000
February	988,000	August	700,000
March	1,140,000	September	900,000
April	1,150,000	October	963,000
May (base)	940,000	November	1,200,000
June	680,000	December	1,425,000

Answer:
Procedure: Divide each month's spending by $9,400 (base ÷ 100).

Month	Spending	Index
January	$ 300,000	32
February	988,000	105
March	1,140,000	121
April	1,150,000	122
May	940,000	100
June	680,000	72
July	654,000	70
August	700,000	74
September	900,000	96
October	963,000	102
November	1,200,000	128
December	1,425,000	152

Interpretation: March, April, November, and December are substantially higher spending months, with December 52% above May spending. January is the lowest month of spending and is only 32% of the May level.

Chapter 4 Review Problems

1. Monday through Friday, 6 to 10 AM, fifteen radio stations have the following average 1/4 hour audience (adults 18+years of age). Index the stations to the base of Station H.

Station	Audience	Index
A	101,500	_____
B	79,300	_____
C	68,000	_____
D	50,400	_____
E	48,500	_____
F	36,400	_____
G	32,300	_____
H (base)	31,700	_____
I	28,100	_____
J	19,800	_____
K	18,600	_____
L	18,100	_____
M	16,000	_____
N	13,900	_____
O	13,500	_____

2. The average 1/4 hour adult audience, Monday through Sunday, 6
   AM to midnight, for fifteen radio stations is 28,140. Determine
   the index of each station to the base of 28,140.

Station	Audience	Index
A	44,700	_____
B	47,200	_____
C	48,300	_____
D	47,100	_____
E	21,300	_____
F	25,200	_____
G	27,300	_____
H	34,800	_____
I	27,900	_____
J	19,000	_____
K	12,600	_____
L	19,800	_____
M	13,000	_____
N	16,400	_____
O	16,600	_____
base	28,140	100

3. Using 1980 as the base year, index Brand X advertising for each year shown below.

Year	Advertising	Index
1975	$3,538,200	_____
1976	2,891,000	_____
1977	3,275,500	_____
1978	3,469,300	_____
1979	3,743,100	_____
1980 (base)	4,101,900	_____
1981	4,256,800	_____
1982	4,009,500	_____
1983	4,624,300	_____
1984	4,907,600	_____
1985	5,839,700	_____

4. Based on the data in 3, above, what is the percent increase in advertising spent in 1985 compared to 1980?

5. Based on the data in 3, above, what is the percent decrease in expenditure for 1976 compared to 1980?

5

Indexing Product Usage Profile

The preceding chapter explains indexing to a base number to which you want all other numbers compared, such as comparing yearly sales to a base year, or comparing monthly expenditures to an average month. Another popular use of indexing compares the product usage profile to the profile of the population.

If we know nothing about a product's demographic profile, we might assume that its demographic characteristics (like age, sex, income, family size, etc.) parallel the U.S. population. For example, 56% of the U.S. population is in the age group of 25 to 54, so a universally used product would also show 56% of its users to be 25 to 54 years of age. But what if a particular product has 70% of its users in the 25 to 54 age group? An index relating the actual percentage (70%) to the population percentage (56%) will add perspective to the number.

$$\frac{70\% \text{ (percent of product users who are age 25-54)}}{56\% \text{ (percent of population who are age 25-54)}} \times 100$$

$$= 125 \text{ Index, Users age 25-54}$$

In this case, the product has an index of 125 for adults 25–54. The index quickly tells us that the product is 25% above what we might expect relative to the population.

Formula

$$\text{Index number} = \frac{\% \text{ of users in a demographic segment}}{\% \text{ of population in the same segment}} \times 100$$

Points to Remember

- Indices should be expressed as whole numbers.

- A *product usage index* assumes that the U.S. population represents the "norm" or base of "100".

- The demographic segment with the highest index number does not necessarily represent the best potential.

Despite a high product usage index, a demographic segment may have a small population size, a low percentage of total sales, or a low share of total product usage. A high index is not reason enough to select a demographic target. First, examine the percent or relative volume of sales or product usage. Second, consider the size of the demographic segment. It may be advantageous to select a demographic target with a larger population or higher product usage even though the segment may have a lower index.

Product User Information

Product user information, like that contained in the following table, might be extracted from proprietary studies or from syndicated research such as *Mediamark Research Inc. (MRI)* or *Simmons Market Research Bureau (SMRB)*.

Purchasers of Regular Size Candy Bars

Demographic Segment	Total U.S. Population (thousands)	(%)	Purchasers of Candy Bars (thousands)	(%)	INDEX
All Adults	174,900	100.0	117,600	67.2	100
Men	83,400	47.7	52,700	44.8	94
Women	91,500	52.3	64,900	55.2	106
Graduated College	30,500	17.4	19,600	16.7	96
Attended College	31,600	18.1	22,100	18.8	104
Graduated High School	68,400	39.1	47,400	40.3	103
Did Not Grad. H.S.	44,400	25.4	28,500	24.2	95
18-24	27,100	15.5	20,400	17.3	112
25-34	42,400	24.2	32,000	27.2	112
35-44	32,400	18.6	23,100	19.6	105
45-54	22,900	13.1	14,000	11.9	91
55-64	22,600	12.9	13,500	11.5	89
65 or Over	27,500	15.7	14,600	12.5	80
Employed Full-Time	98,600	56.4	67,800	57.7	102
Part-Time	11,100	6.3	7,900	6.7	106
Not Employed	65,200	37.3	41,900	35.6	95
Hshld Inc $50,000+	36,600	20.9	24,100	20.5	98
$40,000-49,999	24,300	13.9	16,400	13.9	100
$35,000-39,999	14,900	8.5	10,400	8.8	104
$25,000-34,999	32,300	18.5	22,500	19.1	103
$15,000-24,999	32,900	18.8	22,600	19.2	102
Less Than $15,000	33,900	19.4	21,600	18.4	95

Example 1:

According to the table, what is the index of candy bar purchases among adult women, and what does the index mean? Show the mathematics followed to derive the index.

Answer:
Adult women purchasers have an index of 106. The index means that adult women purchase six percent more candy bars than might be expected based on their proportion of the U.S. population.

$$\frac{55.2\% \text{ (percentage of candy bar purchases by adult women)}}{52.3\% \text{ (percentage of population who are adult women)}} \times 100$$

$$= 106 \text{ Index, Adult Women Purchasers of Candy Bars}$$

Example 2:

According to the table above, what is the index of candy bar purchases among adults 25-34, and what does the index mean? Show the mathematics followed to derive the index.

Answer:
Adults 25-34 have an index of 112 for purchasing candy bars.

The index means that 25-34 year old adults purchase 12% more candy bars than might be expected based on their proportion of the U.S. population.

$$\frac{27.2\% \text{ (percent of candy bar purchases by 25-34 year olds)}}{24.2\% \text{ (percent of population who are adults 25-34)}} \times 100$$

$$= 112 \text{ Index, 25-34 year old purchasers of Candy Bars}$$

Example 3:

According to the table above, what is the index of candy bar purchase among adults 65 or older, and what does the index mean? Show the mathematics followed to derive the index.

Answer:
Adults 65 or older have an index of 80 for purchasing candy bars.

The index means that adults 65 or older purchase only 80% of the candy bars that might be expected based on their proportion of the U.S. population. Putting it another way, adults 65 or older purchase 20% less than their proportion of the population (100% − 80% = 20% less than the norm).

$$\frac{12.5\% \text{ (percent of candy bar purchases by 65 + adults)}}{15.7\% \text{ (percent of population who are adults 65 +)}} \times 100$$

$$= 80 \text{ Index, Adults 65 + purchasing Candy Bars}$$

Example 4:   According to the table above, what three classifications are reported for "employment status"? What is the index reported for each employment segment, and what is wrong with targeting that segment with the highest index?

Answer:
The three segments and their product usage index are as follows:

Employed Full-Time	102 Index
Part-Time	106 Index
Not Employed	95 Index

"Employed part-time" has the highest product usage index (106), but the segment represents only 6.3% of the population and 6.7% of candy bar purchases. The segment of "employed full-time" has almost as high an index (102) and represents 58% of the candy bar purchases. Because the "not employed" segment represents more than a third of the usage (35%) and has a 95 index, there is little value to selecting employment status at all for target audience selection.

Chapter 5 Review Problems

1. Following are demographic data on U.S. population by gender for widget product usage.

Demographic Segment	Total U.S. Population (%)	Widget Users (%)
Men	47.7	65.3
Women	52.3	34.7

A. What is the product usage index for men? _____

B. What is the product usage index for women? _____

C. Is the population skewed heavier toward men or women? _____

D. Is the product skewed heavier toward men or women? _____

2. Calculate the Index for widget product usage in each of the following demographic segments of age.

Demographic Segment	Total U.S. Population (%)	Widget Users (%)	Index
18–24	15.5	12.9	_____
25–34	24.2	23.3	_____
35–44	18.6	24.2	_____
45–54	13.1	16.5	_____
55–64	12.9	13.4	_____
65 or over	15.7	9.7	_____

3. If a marketing judgment required an index of 120 or better to justify advertising emphasis, what age bracket would receive emphasis per the above table?

Ages _____ to _____

4. Calculate the index for widget product usage in each of the following demographic segments of income.

Demographic Segment	Total U.S. Population (%)	Widget Users (%)	Index
Hshld Inc $50,000+	20.9	20.5	_____
$40,000–49,999	13.9	16.1	_____
$35,000–39,999	8.5	15.3	_____
$25,000–34,999	18.5	19.2	_____
$15,000–24,999	18.8	15.7	_____
Less than $15,000	19.4	13.2	_____

5. If the percentage of "Not employed" widget users is 15% *below* the percentage of "not employed" in the U.S. population, what is the index for "not employed" widget users?

_____

6. If the percentage of widget users who "graduated from college" is 20% *higher* than the percentage of college graduates in the U.S., what is the index for widget users who graduated from college?

_____

7. Since the highest index does not necessarily represent the best demographic segment for "potential", what other characteristics of the demographic should be considered?

A. Percentage of the population,

B. Percentage of total sales,

C. Percentage of product usage,

D. As much marketing information (such as A, B, and C) as is available.

6 Indexing Geographic Sales Profile

This chapter deals with a special kind of index commonly used in *market* selection and in planning geographic strategy. A geographic "market" may be defined as a city, county, state, region, media area (such as a television ADI or DMA), or in any manner which provides physical, measurable, boundaries. Like the *product usage demographic profile* covered in the previous chapter, the *geographic sales profile* is indexed against a base of the U.S. population.

If we know nothing about a product's geographic sales profile, we might assume that its market-by-market sales will parallel the U.S. population. For example, 14% of the U.S. population is concentrated in the five Pacific States of Alaska, Washington, Oregon, California, and Hawaii, so a universally used product would also have 14% of its sales in the Pacific. But what if a particular product has 28% of its sales in the Pacific region? An index relating the actual percentage (28%) to the population percentage (14%) will add perspective to the number.

$$\frac{28\% \text{ (percent of product sales in the Pacific)}}{14\% \text{ (percent of population in the Pacific)}} \times 100$$

$$= 200 \text{ Index, Users in the Pacific Region}$$

In this case, the product has an index of 200 for the Pacific Region. The index quickly tells us that the product is 100% above the "norm" of 100, where "100" represents what we might expect based on the distribution of population.

Brand Development Index (BDI) and Category Development Index (CDI)

Individual market "Product Sales" may be viewed by specific "brand" or by total "category" of competing brands. To illustrate the difference between brands and categories, consider that Hershey and Nestlé are brands in the candy bar category, Skippy and Jif are brands in the peanut butter category, Serta and Simmons are brands in the mattress category.

Brand Development Index (BDI) relates the percent of a brand's sales in a market to the percent of the U.S. population in that same market.

Category Development Index (CDI) relates the percent of a Category's sales in a market to the percent of the U.S. population in that same market.

Formula

$$BDI = \frac{\% \text{ of a Brand's Total U.S. Sales in ``Market X''}}{\% \text{ of the Total U.S. Population in ``Market X''}} \times 100$$

$$CDI = \frac{\% \text{ of a Category's Total U.S. Sales in ``Market X''}}{\% \text{ of the Total U.S. Population in ``Market X''}} \times 100$$

Points to Remember

- Indexes should be expressed as whole numbers.

- BDI and CDI assume that the U.S. population represents the "norm" or base of "100."

- Markets with the highest index numbers do not necessarily represent the best potential.

Despite a high BDI or CDI, a market may have a small population size, a low percentage of total sales, or a low share of total product usage. A high index is not reason enough to select a market for advertising or emphasis. First, examine the percent or relative volume of sales or product usage. Second, consider the size of the market. It may be advantageous to select a market with a larger population or higher product usage even though the market may have a lower index.

Market Information and Sales Indexes

Population information by market is available from a number of syndicated sources, including *Sales and Marketing Management Magazine: Survey of Buying Power*, and *Standard Rate and Data Service*, as well as various government and commercial reference sources. Regional population data is reported in *Mediamark Research Inc.* (MRI) and *Simmons Market Research Bureau* (SMRB) syndicated studies. Brand and category sales information by market, however, generally comes from proprietary and specific industry studies. The following table is a typical composite of population, brand, and category sales information.

Geographic Sales Profile, Hypothethical Brand and Category

Rank	TV Market	U.S. Population (%)	Brand Sales (%)	BDI	Category Sales (%)	CDI
1	New York	7.6	20.9	275	6.9	91
2	Los Angeles-Palm Springs	5.4	2.4	44	4.8	89
3	Chicago	3.6	5.1	142	4.9	136
4	Philadelphia	3.0	3.2	107	3.0	100
5	San Francisco-Oakland	2.3	1.4	61	2.1	91
6	Boston	2.3	4.5	196	2.2	96
7	Washington DC	1.9	3.9	205	2.0	105
8	Detroit	1.8	1.0	56	1.7	94
9	Dallas-Fort Worth	1.8	.9	50	2.2	122
10	Cleveland	1.6	2.5	156	1.7	106
11	Houston	1.6	.4	25	.8	50
12	Atlanta	1.4	.5	36	1.3	93
13	Minneapolis-St. Paul	1.4	1.5	107	1.1	79
14	Seattle-Tacoma-Bellingham	1.3	.7	54	1.2	92
15	Miami	1.3	1.2	92	1.5	115
16	Pittsburgh	1.2	0	0	0	0
17	St. Louis	1.2	1.0	83	1.0	83
18	Tampa-St. Petersburg	1.2	1.1	92	1.4	117
19	Sacramento-Stockton	1.0	.6	60	.9	90
20	Denver	1.0	2.1	210	1.1	110
21	Baltimore	1.0	.6	60	1.1	110
22	Phoenix	1.0	1.6	160	1.3	130
23	Hartford-New Haven	1.0	2.5	250	1.1	110
24	San Diego	.9	.5	56	.8	89
25	Orlando-Daytona Beach	.9	1.1	122	1.0	111
	TOTAL	48.7	61.2	126	47.1	97

BDI and CDI are important considerations in planning geographic strategy and in market selection. The relative importance of BDI versus CDI changes with the situation.

High BDI and high CDI usually means excellent sales opportunities for both the brand and the category. This kind of profile is sought after for market emphasis (see Pheonix and Chicago).

High BDI and low CDI reveals that the brand is doing well in spite of less success for the composite of all brands in the category. This condition requires investigation to assure that further category decline will not erode brand sales. Emphasis to protect your brand leadership is also worth considering (see Minneapolis-St. Paul and New York in the table).

Low BDI and high CDI suggests that the brand is facing difficulties that other brands do not seem to have. High priority should be given to analysis of the market to see if the brand can be revitalized and obstacles overcome. The high CDI can reflect a wide base of average users or a concentrated base of loyal heavy users of competitive brands (see Dallas-Fort Worth and Baltimore in the table).

Low BDI and low CDI is the least desired profile. The cost of turning this profile around is usually not worth the effort (see Pittsburgh and Houston in the table).

The actual process of selecting markets for advertising emphasis often begins by setting judgment standards, such as the following:
- Only markets with a BDI of 130 or higher will be considered.
- Only markets with a BDI 10 points larger than the CDI will be considered.
- Marketing criteria, such as...
  —a minimum percent or dollar growth in annual sales,
  —a minimum market size or share of sales,
  —a history of competitive advertising activity.

BDI and CDI should not be the only considerations for market selection or advertising emphasis.

Example 1:

According to the table, Washington DC accounts for 1.9% of the U.S. population. The brand derives 3.9% of its sales from the market. Show the mathematical process followed to derive the BDI.

Answer:

$$\frac{3.9\% \text{ (percent of U.S. brand sales in Washington DC)}}{1.9\% \text{ (percent of U.S. population in Washington DC)}} \times 100$$

$$= 205 \text{ BDI}$$

Example 2: According to the table, 2.0% of the brand category sales take place in Washington DC. Show the mathematical process followed to derive the CDI.

Answer:

$$\frac{2.0\% \text{ (percent of U.S. category sales in Washington DC)}}{1.9\% \text{ (percent of U.S. population in Washington DC)}} \times 100$$
$$= 105 \text{ CDI}$$

Example 3: Why does Pittsburgh have a zero BDI and CDI?

Answer:

Pittsburgh reports zero sales for both the brand and the category. No BDI or CDI can be calculated.

Example 4: Boston has a BDI of 196 and a CDI of 96. Explain the meaning and implication of these two indexes.

Answer:

The BDI of 196 reveals that Boston accounts for almost twice as much brand sales as might be expected based on its share of the U.S. population. It is 96% over the "norm" base of 100.

The CDI of 96 indicates that Boston is a fairly typical market for sales of the entire category. It is just 4% under the "norm" of 100 (100% − 96% = 4%).

The condition of a high BDI and a much lower CDI suggests that the brand is enjoying some favored response by product users, and consideration should be given to protecting the advantage with emphasis advertising.

Chapter 6 Review Problems

Following is U.S. population, with hypothetical brand sales and category sales data for five markets.

TV Market	U.S. Population (%)	Brand Sales (%)	Category Sales (%)
New York	7.6	11.4	6.5
Los Angeles-Palm Springs	5.4	6.5	6.4
Chicago	3.6	2.8	4.7
Boston	2.3	2.2	2.3
Atlanta	1.4	2.8	2.0

1. What is the brand development index for each of the five markets?

   New York   _____

   Los Angeles-Palm Springs   _____

   Chicago   _____

   Boston   _____

   Atlanta   _____

2. What is the category development index for each of the five markets?

   New York   _____

   Los Angeles-Palm Springs   _____

   Chicago   _____

   Boston   _____

   Atlanta   _____

3. Which of the five markets has the highest BDI?

   _____

   If you could provide emphasis in only one market, why might another market be more likely to receive the emphasis?

   _____

   _____

4. Looking at Chicago's BDI and CDI, what concerns might a media planner consider?

_____

_____

_____

5. Looking at the BDI, CDI, and share of sales for Los Angeles, what can be assumed about the market's potential?

_____

_____

_____

7 Averages

An average is a number that is typical of a group of numbers or quantities. The most common average used in media calculations is the *mean,* or arithmetic average, but there may be occasions when you may need to find the *median* or the *mode.*

Mean

Mean is the sum of a group of quantities divided by the number of quantities. For example, the average, or mean, of 4, 5, 6, 7, and 8 is 6.

$$
\begin{array}{r}
4 \\
5 \\
6 \\
7 \\
+\ 8 \\
\hline
30 \div 5 = 6
\end{array}
$$

Using your calculator, this would be a chain calculation. If your calculator has an *item count* key, you may use it to count the number of quantities to be divided into the sum.

Here are two more examples in finding the mean:

Example 1:   Find the mean for the following set of numbers.
10, 12, 13, 15, 10, 5, 5.

Answer:
$$
\begin{array}{r}
10 \\
12 \\
13 \\
15 \\
10 \\
5 \\
+\ 5 \\
\hline
70 \div 7 = 10
\end{array}
$$

Example 2:   A six-year history of advertising spending is provided below. What is the average (mean) year's advertising expenditure?

	(000)
1980	$3,720
1981	3,600
1982	4,250
1983	5,051
1984	5,825
1985	5,154

Answer: Sum of expenditures $27,600,000 ÷ 6 (years) = $4,600,000 average.

Advantage

The mean is consistent with the total of the set of numbers being averaged. The total can always be derived if given the mean and the number of items in the set. This relationship to the total does not exist for the median and mode.

Disadvantage

If extreme values occur in a series of numbers or quantities, the mean may lead us to a false impression of that set of numbers. For example, a salesman's salary history for five years is shown below. Because of the extreme salary in one year, the mean gives a false impression of his typical salary.

$$
\begin{array}{r}
\$18,200 \\
60,300 \\
17,800 \\
18,300 \\
18,700 \\
\hline
\$133,300 \div 5 = \$26,660 \text{ average}
\end{array}
$$

56

Median

The median is the number that occupies the middle position when numbers are arranged in their natural order, either least to greatest or greatest to least. There are just as many numbers above the median as there are below the median.

When a set of numbers contains an even number of members, there is no middle number. In this case, we usually give the mean of the two middle numbers as the median.

The median is not influenced by extreme values. However, be alert that dispersion of values in a set of numbers can make the median a poor representation of the set as a whole.

Here are three examples in finding the median.

Example 1:

Find the median of the following set of numbers: 9, 7, 5, 4, 3, 2, 1.

Answer:
```
      9
      7
      5
───▶  4      4 is the median
      3
      2
      1
```

Example 2:

Find the median of the following set of numbers: 125, 136, 300, 136, 210, 200, 286, 100, 240.

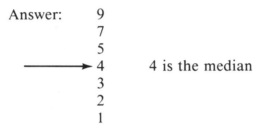

Answer:
```
      100
      125
      136
      136
───▶  200      200 is the median
      210
      240
      286
      300
```

Example 3:

Find the median of the following set of numbers: 17, 19, 23, 25, 28, 31.

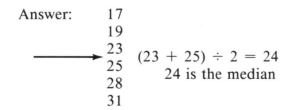

Answer:
```
      17
      19
      23
───▶         (23 + 25) ÷ 2 = 24
      25        24 is the median
      28
      31
```

Mode

The mode is the number that occurs most frequently in a set of numbers. If no number occurs more than once, the mode does not exist (there is no mode). If two or more numbers occur an equal number of times, there can be more than one mode for that set of numbers.

The mode is the least used average, and for most media applications, the mean or median will better represent a set of numbers. For example, in the series 3, 3, 5, 6, 7, 8, 24, the mode is 3 and is less typical of the set then the median (6) or the mean (8). Should you desire a better understanding of the mode, following are four examples.

Example 1:

Find the mode of the following numbers:
81, 85, 85, 89, 90, 91, 95.

Answer: 85 is the mode. It occurs twice in the series.

Example 2:

Find the mode of the following numbers:
41, 41, 48, 10, 12, 12, 16, 12.

Answer: 12 is the mode. It occurs three times in the series, which is more frequently than any other number.

Example 3:

Find the mode of the following numbers:
2, 2, 25, 7, 7, 11, 27.

Answer: This set has two modes, 2 and 7. Each occurs twice, so the series is bi-modal.

Example 4:

Find the mode of the following numbers:
5, 11, 17, 32, 46.

Answer: Each number occurs only once, so there is no mode.

**Chapter 7 Review
Problems**

1. Find the mean (arithmetic average), the median, and the mode for the following sets of numbers.

A. 54, 89, 76, 23, 54, 71, and 95.

B. 68, 29, 59, 55, and 29.

C. 571, 376, 489, 624, and 840.

D. 3.65, 3.7, 3.7, 12.18, 9.1, 8.06, and 9.1.

E. $979, $657, $784, $916, $872, and $784.

2. Brand X's monthly advertising spending is listed below. What is the average (mean) monthly spending?

January	$ 300,000	July	$ 654,000
February	988,000	August	712,000
March	1,140,000	September	900,000
April	1,150,000	October	963,000
May	940,000	November	1,200,000
June	692,000	December	1,425,000

3. The eleven–year history of a client's sales shows overall growth. What is the average year (mean) sales for the period?

Year	Sales
1975	$3,638,200
1976	2,891,000
1977	3,275,500
1978	3,463,300
1979	3,744,100
1980	4,101,900
1981	4,256,800
1982	4,009,500
1983	4,624,300
1984	4,907,600
1985	5,829,200

4. Fifteen people comprised an advertising test panel. What was the average (mean) age, and what was the median income?

Panel Member	Age	Income
A	42	$32,600
B	35	18,400
C	41	23,100
D	44	27,200
E	37	15,900
F	36	30,500
G	42	25,700
H	39	30,000
I	40	28,400
J	36	22,700
K	40	19,300
L	36	31,600
M	35	14,900
N	38	26,800
O	44	43,500

5. What is the average income of the panel in problem 4?

8 Weighting

Weighting is a method of adjusting numbers to reflect additional considerations or value modifiers. The applied weights may be in the form of an index, percent, fraction, or ratio. The weight is multiplied times the number to obtain a "weighted" quantity or number.

Weighted numbers no longer represent an exact count or measurement. Their purpose is to reflect a value measure that can be compared with other weighted numbers.

Suppose you are comparing two magazines strictly on the basis of audience size, but research tells you that males purchase only half as much of your product as do females. Which magazine provides the largest unweighted audience? The largest weighted audience?

	Magazine A			Magazine B		
	Male	Female	Total	Male	Female	Total
Unweighted Audience (000)	3,200	4,800	8,000	1,700	5,800	7,500
Weight (% value)	50%	100%		50%	100%	
Weighted Audience (000)	1,600	4,800	6,400	850	5,800	6,650

On an unweighted basis, you would choose Magazine A because it delivers 500,000 more unadjusted audience. However, Magazine B is the better choice because it provides 250,000 more weighted audience after discounting male readers by 50%.

Note that weights used to adjust media audiences usually should not exceed a 100 index or 100%. This precaution prevents ending up with a weighted audience numbering more than the population. It also directionally reflects the effect of refinements, that is, the elimination of wasted audience and the discounting of less effective exposures should diminish the audience size.

More than one weight adjustment can be applied to a measurement such as audience. For example, one adjustment may represent *noticing* potential (the probability of the ad to be seen); a second adjustment may represent *communication* (support provided by elements like compatible editorial). Since weights are applied by multiplication, they may be applied in any order.

$$\text{Audience} \times \text{Weight 1} \times \text{Weight 2} = 100 \times .80 \times .60 =$$
$$80.00 \times .60 = 48$$

or

$$\text{Weight 1} \times \text{Weight 2} \times \text{Audience} = .80 \times .60 \times 100 =$$
$$.48 \times 100 = 48$$

or

$$\text{Weight 1} \times \text{Audience} \times \text{Weight 2} = .80 \times 100 \times .60 =$$
$$80.00 \times .60 = 48$$

or

$$\text{Weight 2} \times \text{Audience} \times \text{Weight 1} = .60 \times 100 \times .80 =$$
$$60.00 \times .80 = 48$$

Following are two exercises in the application of weights.

Example 1: Choose the single best television package given the following information:

	Package A	Package B	Package C
Women 18-34	134,706	129,796	143,640
Women 35-54	103,620	105,240	102,600
Women 55+	107,074	115,764	95,760
Men 18+	248,864	251,732	255,376
Total Adults 18+	594,264	602,532	597,376

The following weights have been agreed to by the client and agency:

Women 18-34	100 Index
Women 35-54	75 Index
Women 55+	50 Index
Men 18+	Zero Value

All these schedules have the same cost, programming mix, schedule spread, etc.

Answer:

	Unweighted		Weight		Weighted
	(000)				**(000)**
Package A					
W18-34	134,706	×	1.00	=	134,706
W35-54	103,620	×	.75	=	77,715
W55+	107,074	×	.50	=	53,537
Men	248,864	×	0	=	0
Total	594,264				265,958
Package B					
W18-34	129,796	×	1.00	=	129,796
W35-54	105,240	×	.75	=	78,930
W55+	115,764	×	.50	=	57,882
Men	251,732	×	0	=	0
Total	602,532				266,608
Package C					
W18-34	143,640	×	1.00	=	143,640
W35-54	102,600	×	.75	=	76,950
W55+	95,760	×	.50	=	47,880
Men	255,376	×	0	=	0
Total	597,376				268,470

Package C has the largest weighted audience and therefore, the greatest value, given the assigned value weights.

Example 2: Determine which media schedule provides the largest weighted audience.

Schedule A has an unadjusted audience of 300,000,000.
    It has a noticing weight of 0.50.
    It has a communication weight of 0.70.

Schedule B has an unadjusted audience of 150,000,000.
 It has a noticing weight of 0.63.
 It has a communication weight of 1.00

Answer:

	Schedule A	Schedule B
Unweighted Audience	300,000,000	150,000,000
Noticing Weight	x .50	x .63
Post-Noticing Audience	150,000,000	94,500,000
Communication Weight	x .70	x 1.00
Weighted Audience	105,000,000	94,500,000

Schedule A has the largest weighted audience.

Additional considerations for establishing value weights are discussed in chapter ten, entitled "Cognitive Analysis—The Importance of Thought in Interpreting Qualitative Data." If you are assigning weights to qualitative measurements, chapter ten points out the dangers of the method becoming the key discriminator rather than the values you intend to consider.

Chapter 8 Review Problems

1. An agency is evaluating six women's magazines. Using the index provided, weight the audience of each magazine to reflect the amount of food editorial carried.

Magazine	Audience (Women 18+)	Weight (Index based on) (% of Food Edit)	Weighted Audience
	(000)		(000)
A	17,171	58	_____
B	17,827	61	_____
C	18,367	83	_____
D	12,398	58	_____
E	13,274	61	_____
F	17,200	100	_____

2. If adults over 34 years of age consume snack chips at 40% of the per capita rate of those 18 to 34, what is the weighted audience for each of the following radio stations?

Station	Adult Audience Avg. 1/4 Hour	Age Distribution 18-34	35 +	Weighted Audience
A	53,600	30%	70%	_____
B	51,800	32%	68%	_____
C	44,200	21%	79%	_____
D	39,600	26%	74%	_____
E	31,300	52%	48%	_____

Station	Adult Audience Avg. 1/4 Hour	Age Distribution 18-34	35 +	Weighted Audience
F	26,200	83%	17%	_____
G	23,500	75%	25%	_____
H	21,200	27%	73%	_____
I	18,200	86%	14%	_____
J	17,700	46%	54%	_____

Hint: The weighted audience for Station A is (53,600 × 30%) + (53,600 × 70% × 40%). The memory function of a calculator (see chapter one) can combine the two age calculations without re-entering the data.

3. The product to be advertised is an ingredient used only in baking desserts. Given the number of dessert recipes for the average issue of each magazine, index the recipe count (Magazine E = 100 index), and weight each magazine's audience based on the recipe index.

Magazine	Audience (Women 18+)	Dessert Recipes Number in Avg. Issue	Index	Weighted Audience
	(000)			(000)
A	17,171	2	_____	_____
B	17,827	8	_____	_____
C	18,367	5	_____	_____
D	12,398	3	_____	_____
E	13,274	15	_____	_____
F	17,200	10	_____	_____

4. Two trade journals have a similar target audience circulation and an identical advertising cost. Differences are identified based on reader subscription cost and renewal rate (Weight 1) and editorial environment (Weight 2). What is the weighted target audience for each journal?

	Journal A	Journal B
Unweighted Audience	109,000	112,000
Weight 1 (Indexed)	100	85
Weight 2 (Indexed)	92	100
Weighted Audience		

9

CPM

CPM is the abbreviation for *cost per thousand.* It is the method of relating circulation or audience to cost. It is a common denominator for media comparisons, and one of several criteria usually considered in the media selection process.

Calculating CPM

CPM is determined by dividing media circulation or audience into the media cost times 1000. More simply, move the decimal point of the circulation or audience three places to the left and divide into the media cost.

$$\text{CPM} = (\text{Cost} \times 1000) \div \text{Audience}$$
or
$$\text{CPM} = \text{Cost} \div \frac{\text{Audience}}{1000}$$

Because cost can be related to various circulation and audience measurements, CPM can be no more significant or discriminating than the measurement selected. Consequently, media cost analysis should strive for the closest possible measurement of the effective target audience achievable. This means eliminating unwanted audience or waste, and the discounting or weighting of lesser important segments of the audience. Weighting may also consider the probability of commercial noticing and may even reflect probability of communication. The more discriminating the measurement of audience, the more discriminating will be the CPM. Look at the illustration below.

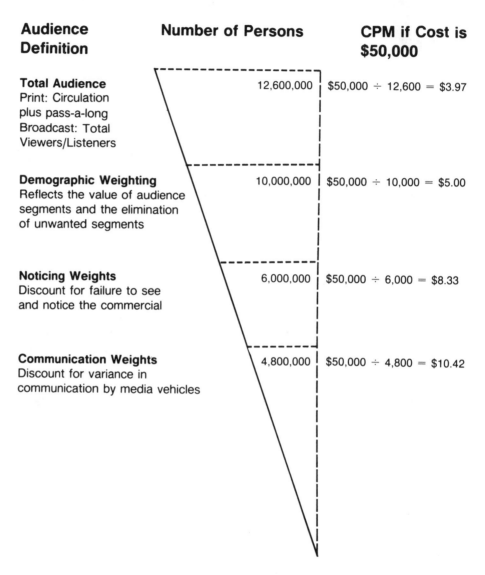

Audience Definition	Number of Persons	CPM if Cost is $50,000
Total Audience Print: Circulation plus pass-a-long Broadcast: Total Viewers/Listeners	12,600,000	$50,000 ÷ 12,600 = $3.97
Demographic Weighting Reflects the value of audience segments and the elimination of unwanted segments	10,000,000	$50,000 ÷ 10,000 = $5.00
Noticing Weights Discount for failure to see and notice the commercial	6,000,000	$50,000 ÷ 6,000 = $8.33
Communication Weights Discount for variance in communication by media vehicles	4,800,000	$50,000 ÷ 4,800 = $10.42

Remember that CPM, even on a weighted audience basis, simply relates cost and audience. It does not reflect the configuration of audience in terms of size or reach, frequency, or continuity. Consequently, it should seldom be used as the only criterion for media selection.

Following are three examples in solving for CPM.

Example 1:

Given the circulation and cost of two magazines, determine their CPM.

Magazine	Circulation	Pg. 4 Color Cost
Magazine A	7,010,192	$69,600
Magazine B	6,201,777	$59,830

Answer:

Magazine	Cost		Circulation ÷ 1000		CPM
Magazine A	$69,600	÷	7,010,192	=	$9.93
Magazine B	$59,830	÷	6,201,777	=	$9.65

Note that Magazine B has a lower circulation CPM, but we know nothing about the size of the target audience or the communication potential of our specific advertising.

Example 2:

Given the demographically weighted target audience, the noticing/communication weight adjustment, and the cost, determine each magazine's weighted CPM.

Magazine	Demographically Weighted Audience	Noticing/ Communication Weight	Page 4-C Cost
Magazine A	15,210,720	.37	$69,600
Magazine B	13,857,800	.32	$59,830

Answer:

Magazine	Demographically Weighted Audience		Noticing/ Communication Weight		Total Weighted Audience
Magazine A	15,210,720	×	.37	=	5,627,966
Magazine B	13,857,800	×	.32	=	4,434,496

Magazine	Cost		Weighted Audience ÷ 1,000		CPM
Magazine A	$69,600	÷	5,627.966	=	$12.37
Magazine B	$59,830	÷	4,434.946	=	$13.49

Note that Magazine A becomes the most cost efficient (lowest CPM) on a weighted audience basis. This CPM analysis is based on a single insertion and does not consider audience accumulation potential for a series of insertions or the duplication pattern with other vehicles that might carry the advertising. Again, CPM is only one consideration in media selection.

Example 3: Given three media mixes, their weighted audience (demographically weighted and qualitatively weighted), and their total media cost, determine the CPM of each plan.

Plan (Alt. Media Mix)	Weighted Audience (000)	Media Cost (000)
Plan A	759,856	$9,483
Plan B	690,615	$8,978
Plan C	752,520	$9,256

Answer:

Plan	Media Costs		Weighted Audience ÷ 1,000		CPM
Plan A	$9,483,000	÷	759,856	=	$12.48
Plan B	$8,978,000	÷	690,615	=	$13.00
Plan C	$9,256,000	÷	752,520	=	$12.30

Finding CPM from Cost Per Rating Point

Cost per thousand for a broadcast schedule can be determined from the cost per target audience rating point (abbreviated cost per point or CPP).

Two factors must be known:

1. CPP, which is simply the cost of the schedule divided by the schedule's number of GRPs. (See chapters eight and nine for an explanation of ratings and GRPs.)
2. The total population of the target audience.

The formula for finding CPM from CPP is as follows:

$$CPM = (CPP \times 100) \div \frac{Population}{1000}$$

It often helps to remember a formula if you know how it is derived.

In terms of broadcast media,

$$Cost = CPP \times TRPs$$

and

$$Audience = \frac{TRPS}{100} \times Population$$

The formula for CPM is

$$CPM = Cost \div \frac{Audience}{1000}$$

Substituting broadcast terms into the formula

$$CPM = (CPP \times TRPs) \quad \div \quad \frac{TRPs}{100} \times \frac{Population}{1000}$$

Substituting TRPs = 100*

$$CPM = (CPP \times 100) \quad \div \quad \frac{100}{100} \times \frac{Population}{1000}$$

*Note that TRPs appear on both sides of the division symbol, so they, in effect, cancel out. For mathematical simplicity, it is convenient to assume 100 TRPs.

Following are two examples of finding CPM from CPP.

Example 1:   Network prime time television for a particular period is anticipated to cost $7,000 per point for women 25-54 years of age. There are 45,470,000 women 25-54 years of age in United States TV households. What is the CPM for a schedule of 800 TRPs?

Answer:

$$CPM = (CPP \times 100) \quad \div \quad \frac{Population}{1000}$$

$$CPM = (\$7000 \times 100) \quad \div \quad \frac{45,470,000}{1000}$$

$$CPM = \$700,000 \quad \div \quad 45,470$$

$$CPM = \$15.39$$

You will notice that the goal of 800 TRPs was not used. Had it been utilized, the answer would have been the same.

$$CPM = (CPP \times TRPs) \quad \div \quad \left(\frac{TRPs}{100} \times \frac{Population}{1,000} \right)$$

$$CPM = (\$7,000 \times 800) \quad \div \quad \left(\frac{800}{100} \times \frac{45,470,000}{1000} \right)$$

$$CPM = \$5,600,000 \quad \div \quad 363,760$$

$$CPM = \$15.39$$

Example 2:

Television in a west coast market is expected to cost $204 per point for men 25-54 years of age in fringe time (combination of early and late fringe). The population of men 25-54 years of age is 1,110,000. What is the CPM that should be anticipated for a fringe TV schedule?

Answer:

$$CPM = (CPP \times 100) \div \frac{Population}{1,000}$$

$$CPM = (\$204 \times 100) \div \frac{1,110,000}{1,000}$$

$$CPM = \$20,400 \div 1,110$$

$$CPM = \$18.38$$

Using CPM to Find Cost Per Point

The relationship between CPM and CPP is expressed in the formula:

$$CPM = (CPP \times 100) \div \frac{Population}{1000}$$

Mathematically transposed, the formula can be expressed to find CPP, given CPM and target audience population:

$$\boxed{CPP = CPM \times \frac{Population}{100,000}}$$

Here are two examples of determining CPP from CPM.

Example 1:

Spot radio advertising in a major city is expected to have a CPM of $11.50 for teenagers. Given that the population of teenagers is 830,500, calculate the anticipated cost per point.

Answer:

$$CPP = CPM \times \frac{Population}{100,000}$$

$$CPP = \$11.50 \times \frac{830,500}{100,000}$$

$$CPP = \$11.50 \times 8.305$$

$$CPP = \$95.51$$

Example 2: Daytime television in one city has a CPM of $5.52 among women 18+ years of age. What is the estimated cost per rating point for women, given that the city's adult female population is 725,000?

Answer:

$$CPP = CPM \times \frac{Population}{100,000}$$

$$CPP = \$5.52 \times \frac{725,000}{100,000}$$

$$CPP = \$5.52 \times 7.25$$

$$CPP = \$40.02$$

Milline Rate

The *milline rate* is an archaic cousin of CPM that used to be the basic cost-value measurement for newspapers. It has been almost totally replaced by CPM, but it is included in this manual for historical reference. The milline rate is a CPM that designates the unit of newspaper space as 1000 lines and specifies the audience as circulation.

$$Milline\ rate = Cost\ of\ 1000\ lines \div \frac{Circulation}{1000}$$

Example: Find the milline rate for a newspaper whose circulation is 700,000 and line rate is $4.00 per line.

Answer:

$$Milline\ rate = Cost\ of\ 1000\ lines \div \frac{Circulation}{1000}$$

$$= (\$4.00\ per\ line \times 1000\ lines) \div \frac{700,000}{1,000}$$

$$= \$4,000.00 \div 700$$

$$= \$5.71$$

The obsolescence of the milline rate is reinforced by change in the basic unit of national newspaper advertising space. Ads placed through agencies are usually measured and invoiced in *column inches* (that is, width in standard advertising columns multiplied by the number of inches deep). Ads measured in agate lines are generally confined to local retail advertising, and even then, CPM is the accepted measure of value.

In contrast to the milline rate, remember that CPM can be based on the cost of any size space/commercial length and the audience need not be circulation.

Chapter 9 Review Problems

1. Calculate CPM (based on circulation) for the following seven women's magazines.

Magazine	Circulation	Page 4-Color	CPM
A	7,000,000	$ 75,500	_____
B	8,000,000	$ 88,950	_____
C	5,000,000	$ 74,400	_____
D	5,000,000	$ 57,800	_____
E	6,200,000	$ 71,100	_____
F	3,800,000	$ 51,400	_____
G	6,600,000	$ 71,200	_____

2. Calculate the CPM (based on a given weighted target audience) for the following advertising vehicles.

Medium	Weighted Audience (000)	Ad Cost (space or time)	CPM
Magazine Pg. 4-C	16,965	$ 71,200	_____
Magazine Pg. b/w	16,965	59,500	_____
Net TV Day 30"	5,280	19,000	_____
Net TV Prime 30"	12,195	125,000	_____
Net Radio 60"	1,000	3,250	_____
Newspaper 70 Col In.	25,090	313,600	_____
Outdoor 50 Showing	844,930	1,816,600	_____

3. Daytime network television is expected to cost $3,550 per rating point for adult women. There are 87,480,000 adult women in United States TV households. What is the CPM for a schedule of 200 TRPs?

4. Evening news on network television costs $50,000 for a 30-second commercial, making the cost per rating point $7,940 for adult men. There are 78,870,000 adult men in United States TV households. Determine the CPM.

5. Radio advertising in the top 100 markets costs $7.40 per thousand adult males. Those same 100 markets contain 67,830,000 adult men. What is the cost per rating point (CPP)? Round to the next whole dollar.

6. A network TV sports package costs $8.20 per thousand adult males. There are 78,870,000 adult men in United States TV households. What is the cost per rating point? Round to the next whole dollar.

10 Ratings, Shares, HUTs, and PUTs

These terms are broadcast audience measurements, but since they are also mathematical expressions, they are included in this manual.

Rating is the audience of a particular program or station at a specific period of time expressed as a percent of the audience population. The percent sign is not shown, and the rating may represent household viewing or a specific demographic audience segment's listening or viewing.

Broadcast Medium	Audience (Avg. ¼ Hour)		Population (000)		Rating
Net TV Program for example, Wednesday 9P.M.	18,410,000 HH	÷	83,300,000 TV HH	=	22.1
	4,142,250 M18-34	÷	33,030,000 M18-34	=	12.5
	14,728,000 W18+	÷	86,350,000 W18+	=	17.1
Local Radio Station for example, Monday-Friday 6-10A.M.	56,600 M18+	÷	3,111,900 M18+	=	1.8
	58,200 W18+	÷	3,297,000 W18+	=	1.8
	8,375 M18-34	÷	1,395,900 M18-34	=	.6

The audience and population measurements used to determine individual market ratings can be based on various geographic areas, depending on the medium and rating source.

Television ratings are primarily developed for
    Metro Survey Area (MSA)
    Total Survey Area (TSA)
    Area of Dominant Influence (ADI) as defined by Arbitron
    Designated Market Area (DMA) as defined by A.C. Nielsen

Radio ratings are primarily developed for
    Metro Survey Area (MSA)
    Total Survey Area (TSA)
    Area of Dominant Influence (ADI) as defined by Arbitron

The television areas (ADI and DMA) are frequently the basis for discussions and analyses of all media. They are TV terms applied to broadcast and print media alike.

Share is the audience of a particular television program or time period expressed as a percent of the population viewing TV at that particular time. Share, then, is a percent allocation of the viewing audience and differs from the rating which is a percent of the potential audience. Share is usually reported on a household basis.

HUT or *homes using television* at a particular time, is expressed as a percent of all TV homes. HUT differs from rating because it combines all viewing, rather than identifying specific program viewing.

PUT or persons using television at a particular time, is expressed as a percent of all persons in TV homes. PUT combines all persons viewing, rather than reporting specific program viewing. Note that PUT and *PVT (Persons viewing television)* are interchangeable terms in common usage. A.C. Nielsen continues to use "PUT" and Arbitron has changed to "PVT."

Be aware that the HUT is not necessarily the total of all the household ratings for a specific time period for two reasons.

- Individual program ratings may be excluded because they do not meet the rating service's reporting standards (for example, outside market station spill-in or too small ratings), but that viewing will contribute to the HUT estimate.

- Multi-set homes with simultaneous viewing will contribute to individual program ratings, but contribute only once to the HUT estimate.

The PUT is also not necessarily the total of all of the individual person ratings because the rating service's reporting standards may exclude individual station ratings that still contribute to the PUT estimate.

Ignoring variances caused by rating service reporting standards and multi-set viewing, the following mathematical relationships apply after first converting rating, share, and HUT to decimals.

$$HUT \times Share = Rating\ (HH)$$
$$Rating\ (HH) \div HUT = Share$$
$$Rating\ (HH) \div Share = HUT$$

Example 1:

Thursday nights at 8:30 pm, a TV station enjoys a 40 share. At that time the homes using television (HUT) level is 65. What is the program rating?

Answer:

$$HUT \times Share = Rating\ (HH)$$
$$.65 \times .40 = .26\ or\ 26\ Rating$$

Example 2:

A TV station has a 30 share daily at 2 pm. The program at that time has a 7 rating. What is the HUT level?

Answer:

$$Rating \div Share = HUT$$
$$.07 \div .30 = .23\ or\ 23\ HUT$$

Example 3:

Sunday at 9:30 pm, 68% of the TV households are viewing television. One station has a 20 rating for its movie. What is that station's share?

Answer:

$$Rating \div HUT = Share$$
$$.20 \div .68 = .29\ or\ 29\ Share$$

Chapter 10 Review Problems

1. Determine the rating, given the audience and population. Round to the nearest tenth.

Demographic	Audience	Population	Rating
A. Women 18+	12,427,000	87,480,000	_____
B. Men 18-34	3,885,000	33,200,000	_____
C. Children 2-11	5,216,000	32,600,000	_____
D. Households	16,006,000	83,800,000	_____

2. Based on the average 1/4 hour audience for eight radio stations, what rating does each station possess? The population of adults 18+ years of age is 2,980,000. Round to the nearest tenth.

Station	Audience (Adults 18+) Average ¼ Hour	Rating
A	55,000	_____
B	49,900	_____
C	47,400	_____
D	33,800	_____
E	28,400	_____
F	26,500	_____
G	19,700	_____
H	14,900	_____

3. Find the missing value (rating, share, or HUT), assuming there is no multi-set viewing or unreported viewing. Round to the nearest whole number.

	Rating	Share	HUT
A.	16	32	_____
B.	_____	20	60
C.	9	_____	30
D.	18	33	_____
E.	_____	40	75
F.	5	_____	19

11 GRPs, TRPs, Reach, and Frequency

These media terms express mathematical relationships that warrant discussion in this manual.

Ratings were explained in the previous chapter, and ratings, just like other percentages, can be added as long as they have the same base, that is, all ratings must apply to the same geographic area and reflect the same demographic segment. The aggregate total (the sum) of the ratings is called *Gross Rating Points* or *GRPs*. The sum of the ratings of a specific demographic segment may be called *Target Audience GRPs* or more simply *TRPs*. The term GRPs is generic and may refer to household GRPs or to specific target segment GRPs.

Program	Ratings		
	Household	**Women 18+**	**Men 18-34**
Movie Special	16	16	14
Situation Comedy	22	17	13
Mystery	19	15	11
Total GRPs	57	48	38

In the illustration above, some of the people viewing one of the programs may also view one or more of the other programs. The total of the ratings includes duplication of viewing, hence the name gross rating points.

Just as ratings with the same base can be added, ratings with dissimilar bases should never be added. The abuse of adding dissimilar GRPs is so common a mistake in media advertising that the practice must be exposed to dissuade perpetuation.

Individual market GRPs cannot be added or averaged.

MARKET	TV HOUSEHOLDS	GRPs
Chicago	2,980,000	500
Des Moines	345,000	300

GRPs for the two markets combined are *not* 800 (500 + 300) or 400 (the average of 500 and 300). The base of GRPs is dissimilar. One rating point in Chicago represents 29,800 households; one rating point in Des Moines equals 3,450 households.

To solve the problem:

First, convert the GRPs to a common base, in this case TV households (2,980,000 × 5.00) and (345,000 × 3.00). Remember, GRPs are really a percentage.
$$500 \text{ GRPs} = 500\% \text{ or } 5.00.$$

Second, add the households delivered by the two market schedules.
Finally, divide the number of delivered households by the sum of households in the two markets, and convert back to GRPs by moving the decimal two places to the right.

All three steps in one formula would look like the following problem:

CHICAGO	DES MOINES	TOTAL

$$\frac{(2,980,000 \times 5.00) + (345,000 \times 3.00)}{2,980,000 + 345,000} = 4.79 \text{ or } 479 \text{ GRPs}$$

Note, another approach to the same answer is to weight the GRPs by the size of the individual markets to achieve a common base, and then divide by the sum of the households to determine the average GRPs for the combined area.

$$\frac{(2,980,000 \times 500) + (345,000 \times 300)}{2,980,000 + 345,000} = 479 \text{ average GRPs}$$

GRPs of different demographics cannot be added or averaged:

TARGET	# PERSONS	GRPs
Men	790,000	60
Women	875,000	100

GRPs for total adults is not 160 (60 + 100) or 80 (average of 60 and 100). The base for GRPs is dissimilar. One rating point for men represents 7,900 people, and one rating point for women represents 8,750 people.

To solve the problem: .

First, convert the GRPs to a common base, in this case, the number of persons: (790,000 $\times$ 0.60) and (875,000 $\times$ 1.00).

Second, add the number of men and women delivered by the schedule.

Finally, divide the number of delivered persons by the sum of persons in the market, and convert back to GRPs by moving the decimal two places to the right.

All three steps in one formula would look like the following problem:

MEN	WOMEN	TOTAL PERSONS
$\dfrac{(790,000 \times .60) + (875,000 \times 1.00)}{790,000 + 875,000}$		= .81 or 81 GRPs

Note, another approach to the same answer is to weight the GRPs by the size of the individual segments to achieve a common base, and then divide by the sum of the segments to determine the average GRPs for the combined audience.

MEN	WOMEN	TOTAL PERSONS
$\dfrac{(790,000 \times 60) + (875,000 \times 100)}{790,000 + 875,000}$		= 81 average GRPs

Reach is the number or percent of different homes or persons exposed at least once to an advertising schedule over a specific period of time. Reach, then, excludes duplication.

In the following example, reach among women 18+ years of age could range from 17% (the rating of the largest single audience vehicle) to 48% (assuming no duplication of viewing among the three programs).

Program	Ratings		
	Household	Women 18+	Men 18-34
Movie Special	16	16	14
Situation Comedy	22	17	13
Mystery	19	15	11
Total GRPs	57	48	38

Frequency is the number of times that the average household or person is exposed to the schedule among those persons reached in the specific period of time. Because it is an average frequency, dispersion of frequency of exposure will differ between specific schedules and daypart mixes.

When working with reach and frequency, some rules of thumb should be observed:

- Reach is generally expressed to the closest whole number (no decimals).
- Frequency is generally expressed to the closest tenth (one decimal place).
- Reach and frequency are generally estimated for a four-week or shorter period of time.

The data on which Reach/Frequency models and tables are based are unlikely to support accuracy beyond that recommended in the rules of thumb.

GRPs, reach, and frequency are mathematically related in the following ways:

$$\text{GRPs} = \text{Reach} \times \text{Frequency}$$
$$\text{Reach} = \text{GRPs} \div \text{Frequency}$$
$$\text{Frequency} = \text{GRPs} \div \text{Reach}$$

Media models and Reach/Frequency tables provide estimates of reach and frequency for various schedules. However, given any two factors in the above formula, the third is easily calculated.

Example 1:

An advertising schedule is expected to achieve a four-week reach and frequency of 48%/4.2. What number of GRPs are anticipated to achieve this reach and frequency?

GRPs = Reach × Frequency
GRPs = 48 × 4.2
GRPs = 201.6 or 202 GRPs over four weeks.

Example 2:

A TV schedule of 60 GRPs per week achieves a four-week reach of 83% among men 18+. What is the average frequency of exposure?

Frequency = GRPs (4 weeks) ÷ Reach
Frequency = (60 GRPs × 4 weeks) ÷ 83
Frequency = 2.9

Example 3:

A radio schedule on a relatively small number of stations develops an average frequency of 20 over four-weeks. If the schedule consists of 180 GRPs per week, what reach can be expected?

Reach = GRPs (4 weeks) ÷ Frequency
Reach = (180 GRPs × 4-weeks) ÷ 20
Reach = 720 ÷ 20
Reach = 36%

Chapter 11   Review Problems

1. For the following television schedule, what are the total gross rating points for each demographic segment?

Program	Ratings		
	Household	Women 18+	Women 18-34
Daytime Drama 1	7.9	7.0	4.8
Daytime Drama 2	8.4	7.1	9.2
Daytime Drama 3	7.6	7.2	5.2
News at Noon	7.2	5.7	4.1
Situation Comedy	4.4	3.0	3.6
Game Show 1	6.8	5.2	3.0
Game Show 2	5.2	3.9	3.4
TOTAL GRPs	_____	_____	_____

2. A particular television schedule delivered 400 GRPs among men 25-54 years of age. It also delivered 496 GRPs among men 55+ years of age. How many GRPs were delivered for the combined segment of men 25+ years of age?

The population of men 25-54 = 4,500.
The population of men 55+   = 2,100.

3. Radio advertising GRPs and the population of teenagers (12-17) is provided for three individual markets. What is the combined three market total GRPs?

Market	Teen GRPs	Teen Population
A	600	760,000
B	400	520,000
C	300	410,000

4. Five TV programs have individual ratings of 17, 14, 19, 15, and 12 among adults 18+ years of age. What is the smallest reach and the largest reach possible for a schedule of all five programs?

5. Four daytime TV shows have ratings of 6.2, 3.1, 7.6, and 9.1 among women 18-34 years of age. What is the largest reach and smallest reach possible from a schedule of all four shows?

6. Find the missing values in the chart.

	Reach	Frequency	GRPs
A.	55%	4.6	_____
B.	_____	3.7	259
C.	63%	_____	450
D.	_____	5.4	325
E.	72%	6.1	_____
F.	51%	_____	600

12 Frequency Distribution and Estimating Levels of Effective Frequency

The previous chapter explained that *gross rating points* (GRPs) have two component factors, *Reach* and *Frequency*, and that Frequency is the number of times that the average household or person is exposed to the advertising schedule. This chapter goes a step further and deals with the concept of *frequency distribution*. Frequency distribution recognizes the danger of "averaging" and simply looks closer at how frequency is apportioned among the people exposed to the advertising.

When people ask, "What is dangerous about relying on *average* frequency?" ask if they would be willing to wade across a river that averages only four feet deep. Wouldn't they want to know how deep the river gets at its deepest and how wide it is for that portion that is over four or five feet deep? They may still decide to wade across, but more information reduces the risk. Frequency distribution is the equivalent of a depth report at regular distances across the river. It reduces the risk of misjudgment.

An axiom of "average" in "average frequency", is that some people will see the advertising more than the average and some will see it less than the average. Frequency distribution is a method of reporting "reach" at various levels of frequency. (Remember from Chapter 11 that reach is the number or percentage of different homes or persons exposed at least once to the advertising schedule.)

Frequency distribution is usually too complex to be calculated by hand using formula and a calculator. However, frequency distribution is a common product of media models, especially computerized analysis programs for reach and frequency. Frequency distribution most often takes two forms:

Reach at cumulative levels of frequency,
Reach at individual levels of frequency.

A different schedule, a different daypart, or a different target audience will probably generate a different distribution of frequency. The pattern of distribution for a particular schedule is an estimate based on mathematical projections from known data, no different than the estimates of reach and average frequency. Certain assumptions are made in the media models, such as a "mixture" of program formats and broadcast times. If a particular schedule is concentrated into one time period or one program or program-type, then media model estimates of reach, average frequency, and frequency distribution will be inappropriate.

Example:

A prime time television schedule of 400 GRPs (100 GRPs, Men 18 + , per week for 4 weeks) in a specific market yields a reach of 80% and an average frequency of 5.0. A computerized analysis program estimates the following frequency distribution:

Cumulative Levels of Frequency Distribution		Individual Levels of Frequency Distribution	
# Exposures	Reach %	# Exposures	Reach %
1+	80	1	14
2+	66	2	13
3+	53	3	10
4+	43	4	8
5+	35	5	7
6+	28	6	6
7+	22	7	4
8+	18	8	4
9+	14	9	3
10+	11	10	2
11+	9	11	2
12+	7	12	1

This frequency distribution table estimates the percent of the target audience that is exposed to the advertising one-or-more-times (80%), two-or-more-times (66%), three-or-more-times (53%), etc.

The table also estimates the percent that is exposed to the advertising at individual levels of frequency, i.e. one-time (14%), two-times (13%), three-times (10%), etc. The example boasts a reach of 80% and an average frequency of 5.0. However, the frequency distribution reveals that only 35% of the target will have the opportunity to see the advertising five or more times. Only 53% will be exposed to the ads three or more times. A planner or buyer should next ask, "Is a five frequency necessary? Is a three frequency enough to stimulate response, change an attitude, or prompt a purchase?"

Effective Frequency

Frequency distribution becomes important when experience and/or judgment suggests which levels of frequency are "effective" and (perhaps more realistically) what levels of frequency are *not* effective". Do the people who see only one exposure constitute "wasted impressions"? Does an alternative schedule provide less waste? Referring to the above example, suppose three exposures are necessary to communicate the advertising message. Suddenly, reach (80%) and average frequency (5.0) become meaningless. Only the number of people with a 3 + frequency are important (53% of the target).

How Valid Is a Goal of "3 + Effective Frequency"?

Many studies and much disagreement exist on what constitutes effective frequency. If a consensus exists, it is that individual circumstances—not rules—determine what is "effective." Before you can decide what frequency is effective, you must define your communication objectives. For example, do you want to achieve brand recognition, package recognition, message recall, attitude change, brand preference change, brand purchase or trial? You must evaluate your specific conditions like the strength of your commercial, the complexity of your message, the mind-set of your audience and their perception of your product, and the actions or anticipated reactions of your competition. The list of considerations for determining effective frequency may seem endless, but the greatest concern will be the cost and scarcity of actionable research on which to base a decision.

For lack of better guidance, effective frequency is often assumed to be three or more exposures in a four-week period. Remember that reach, frequency, and frequency distribution are expressions of the "vehicle" exposure and not the specific "ad" exposure. Since fewer people will see or hear a specific ad than will see or hear the program or publication carrying the ad, one "vehicle" exposure is often of little consequence. A 3 + frequency may seem to be a realistic goal. If conditions dictate, such as low awareness, tough competition, and a complex message, then a 4 + or higher effective frequency goal may be selected.

Documenting Effective Frequency with Response Curves

If research resources were unlimited, we could actually measure how many people would respond to one commercial exposure, how many respond to two exposures, to three exposures, etc. Plotted on a graph, the resulting response pattern is called a *Response Curve* or *Response Function*. At some point of incremental frequency, *positive* response will end, and a condition referred to as "commercial wear out" sets in. Perhaps even *negative* response will begin as some people in the audience start forming negative attitudes in reaction and rejection of the advertising content, familiarity, or intensity. Following are two sample illustrations of response curves.

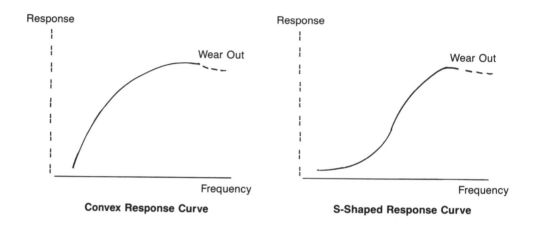

Convex Response Curve   **S-Shaped Response Curve**

Reducing Risk with Frequency Distribution

By requesting and evaluating frequency distribution, the planner reduces the risk and the false security of average frequency. It is possible to see what portion of the audience might be ineffectively reached with only one or two exposures; what portion might be over-exposed with excessive repetition. Alternative schedules and alternative media mixes, appearing equal "on the average", suddenly may have meaningful differences. Frequency distribution can clarify and support media daypart selection, media mix, scheduling strategy, market heavy-up strategy, and budget allocation. Requests for incremental media budget are often founded on frequency distribution analysis. Frequency distribution takes on meaning when it is interpreted with judgments of effective frequency. Once a decision is made on what levels of frequency are effective and what levels are ineffective, compensatory actions can be planned.

Chapter 12 Review Problems

Following are tables of frequency distribution for a television schedule that delivers a reach of 65% and an average frequency of 3.0.

Cumulative Levels of Frequency Distribution		Individual Levels of Frequency Distribution	
# Exposures	Reach (%)	# Exposures	Reach (%)
1+	65	1	19
2+	46	2	13
3+	33	3	10
4+	23	4	8
5+	15	5	6
6+	9	6	4
7+	5	7	2

1. What is the estimated reach that can be delivered with a frequency of two or more times?

   _____

2. What percent of the target is estimated to be reached exactly three times?

   _____

3. If competitive advertising ("share of voice"), the level of your brand's awareness ("share of mind"), and/or the complexity of your message suggest that four or more exposures are needed to be "effective", what is the estimated reach at this effective frequency?

   _____

4. If fewer than two exposures and more than six exposures are judged to be "waste", what is the estimated reach for the effective frequency of two through six?

   _____

5. What is the condition called when incremental frequency fails to generate positive response?

_____

6. What is the name of the pattern depicting "response" plotted against increments of frequency?

_____

7. How can frequency distribution help in the evaluation of alternative schedules and alternative media mix?

_____

_____

_____

13 Media Forecasting: Seasonal Rating Adjustments and Circulation Trending

The ability to predict the future is a skill almost taken for granted among media professionals. No, it is not a requirement that you have supernatural power. It is an expectation that, based on study of past media performance, the media pro will predict future media performance with reasonable accuracy.

Seasonal Rating Adjustments

The weather, seasonal events, and general media usage patterns create predictable seasonal variations in broadcast ratings. If the most recent television rating survey covers May and you want to purchase a schedule for July (when people are often away from the home and viewing is down), or for November (when viewing is high), a seasonal adjustment factor can be calculated and applied to more realistically project the value of the future schedule.

Formula for Television Schedule Projections

Step 1:

$$\frac{\text{Time Period Audience (historic) for Season to be Estimated}}{\text{Latest Time Period Audience for Which You Have Ratings}} \times 100$$

$$= \text{Seasonal Adjustment Factor (\%)}$$

Step 2:

Seasonal Adjustment Factor (%) × Audience (or GRPs) for
Schedule using Current Ratings = Seasonally Adjusted Audience

Example: Estimate Gross Rating Point delivery for a Sacramento Fall 1991 prime time TV schedule (350 GRPs) purchased using May 1991 ratings, and the target demographic is women 18 + .

Step 1:

$$\frac{\text{Persons Viewing Television (PVT),}}{\text{PVT Women 18 + , 8-11 P.M., Nov '90}}{\text{PVT Women 18 + , 8-11 P.M., May 1991}} \times 100$$

$$= \text{Seasonal Adjustment Factor (\%)}$$

$$\frac{43 \text{ PVT Nov '90}}{42 \text{ PVT May '91}} \times 100 = 102\% \text{ Adjustment}$$

Step 2: May to Nov Seasonal Adjustment Factor × 350 GRPs (May 1991 Ratings) = Estimated GRP Delivery, Fall 1991

102% Adjustment × 350 GRPs = 357 GRPs Estimated for Nov 1991

The formula prescribes two steps for making seasonal rating adjustments. Step 1 estimates the amount of change *from* the period for which you have data *to* the period you would like to estimate. Use historic time period data (persons viewing television or average ratings) to determine the percentage of change.

Time period ratings can be extracted from past rating books. For television, the easiest method for determining change is to examine a "Seasonal Variation" study from one of the rating services such as Arbitron or Nielsen. Viewing levels for key rating periods (November, February, May, July) are reported in columnar tables by standard TV dayparts. Markets are listed alphabetically, and average rating levels by standard demographic breaks are listed in columns. An index of change may also be provided.

| | Monday-Friday 8 P.M.–11 P.M. Women 18+ | | | | | | | |
| | Persons Viewing TV | | | | Indices | | | |
Market	NOV	FEB	MAY	JUL	NOV	FEB	MAY	JUL
Sacramento	43	46	42	35	100	107	98	81
San Francisco	47	49	47	37	100	104	100	79

According to the sample table, San Francisco has a July audience that is only 76% of the February audience:

$$\frac{37 \text{ PVT July}}{49 \text{ PVT Feb}} \times 100 = 75.5\% \text{ Adjustment Factor}$$

NOTE: the *indices* in the above table assume November as the base month (100). If projections are being made from the base month, the indices provide the adjustment factor without further calculation. For example, the table shows July is typically 79% of San Francisco's November audience. However, if you want the amount of change from other than the base month, you will have to calculate the percent change (see the February to July calculation above). *Try not to use indices* for calculations because indices themselves are rounded calculations, one step further away from the PVT or average ratings on which they are based.

Step 2 of the formula simply multiplies the adjustment factor obtained in Step 1 times the rating or audience reported by the current rating book. If we purchased a schedule of 400 GRPs using the San Francisco February rating book, it would probably only deliver 302 GRPs in July:

75.5% Adjustment Factor (February to July) × 400 GRPs (Feb)
= 302 GRPs (Estimated July)

CAUTION: the adjustment formula assumes that everything except the size of audience remains constant. This is not a consequential generalization for estimating the delivery of a large schedule. However, it can be disastrously inaccurate for estimating the audience for one program or a narrow daypart. Season to season, programming and advertising adjacencies change! Viewing tastes and programming quality change! As a consequence, daypart generalities are not appropriate for specific rating projections.

**Formula for Individual
Television Program
Projections**

Step 1: Look up the *share* the program received in the latest rating book. If the commercial "spot" is between programs, average the shares for adjacent programming.

Make a judgmental adjustment of the share if competitive programming will change on the future schedule or if the time of broadcast will change from that shown in the current rating book.

If the program is new and not reported in the current rating book, make a judgment of share based on the time period and competitive programming.

Step 2: Multiply the forecasted share (Step 1) times the persons viewing television (PVT) for the season and specific time period being estimated. Remember that share is a percent, and the decimal point must be added whenever share is used in calculations.

Example: Estimate the number of men 18-49 GRPs for a program to run Thursday, 9-10 P.M. on ABC this coming Fall. The most recent rating book for the market is February.

Step 1: Look up the program in the current rating book (Feb.). Let's assume that we find the program received a 12 rating for men 18-49 years of age and a 31 share.

Further checking reveals that the program will run at the same time period in the fall and that counter programming appears to be even weaker than it was in February. Make a judgment of probable share. In this example, we will conservatively estimate a 32 share for Fall.

Step 2: Multiply the forecasted share (32) times the persons viewing television for that time period in Fall. The PVT may be taken from the prior year's rating book or from a rating service seasonal variation study.

Estimated Fall Share × Persons Viewing Television,
Men 18-49, Fall, Thurs 9-10 P.M. = Estimated Fall Rating
.32 × 41 = 13 Estimated Fall Rating

Radio Schedule Projections

Although seasonal variations occur in radio, especially among teen listening during the summer months, the latest rating book covering the season being purchased is usually a realistic projection. Radio ratings tend to be smaller and much more stable than television ratings, so adjustments are of less consequence. In cases where radio formats and station rankings have significantly changed from those in the book on which the schedule was purchased, an adjustment factor can be calculated based on the change in an average quarter-hour rating. As with television, the adjustment factor can be multiplied times the station's audience or GRPs.

Circulation Trending

Magazine circulation owes much of its stability to long-term home and business subscriptions. Notable exceptions to stability are *new* magazines and publications with high individual copy sales. Such exceptions warrant trend analysis and projection.

New Publication Circulation Projections

A new publication often establishes momentum in circulation growth. For example, consider the following circulation trend:

YEAR	Average Paid Circ. for Year	Change Versus Prior Year (%)	
Year #1	1,093,732	—	
Year #2	1,195,978	109	(1,195,978/1,093,732)
Year #3	1,336,247	112	(1,336,247/1,195,978)

It is reasonable to assume that circulation for year #4 will exceed year #3. However, a "formula" for projecting the trend is *not* recommended.

- Look at the circulation of competitive publications. Is the new publication approaching the circulation of competitors'? Is competitors' circulation diminishing with the new publication's growth? Is a continued growth of 12% to 16% realistic?

- Look at the vitality of the publication. Is the editorial as compelling as when it was first published? Are competitors countering with editorial changes that may cancel the editorial distinctions? Are single copy sales continuing to grow?

- Look at the pricing of the publication. Have the subscription and cover prices remained competitive? Have competitors matched pricing and promotional offers?

- Look at the state of the national economy. Circulation for all publications tends to grow in good times and decrease in bad times. Are there external influences on continued growth?

- After studying the above considerations, make a "judgmental" projection of the percentage change in circulation, then multiply that percentage times the current circulation.

114% Projected Change × 1,336,247 Circ, Year #3
= 1,523,322 Estimated Circulation Year #4

Projecting Circulation: Magazines with Heavy Newsstand Sales

Publications which depend heavily on newsstand and grocery store sales for their circulation often show volatility and month-to-month variations. Past circulation is usually reported issue by issue in the *Publisher's Audit Statement* and may resemble the following pattern of a certain women's magazine:

Issue	Total Paid Circ.	15 Issue Av. (%)	Issue	Total Paid Circ.	15 Issue Av. (%)
Jan. 16	4,488,268	96	July 18	4,108,781	88
Feb. 6	4,092,863	88	Aug. 15	4,142,756	89
Mar. 1	4,005,975	86	Sept. 5	4,120,408	89
Mar. 20	4,080,880	88	Oct. 3	5,183,357	111
Apr. 10	4,667,524	100	Oct. 24	5,141,214	111
May 1	4,674,100	100	Nov. 21	5,104,368	110
May 22	4,731,804	102	Dec. 19	5,136,131	110
June 19	6,101,905	131	15 Issue Av.	4,652,022	100

Source: Publisher's Statements, Audit Bureau of Circulation, Dec. 31, 1989 and June 30, 1990.
Author added 15 issue average and percent of average.

102

If a media planner wants to project future circulation for a magazine with heavy single-issue sales, it is reasonable to assume that future circulation patterns may resemble past performance. However once again, a "formula" for projecting the trend is *not* recommended.

- Look at the circulation of competitive publications. Does the pattern appear seasonal and typical?

- Look at the vitality of the publication. Does circulation fluctuate month to month with the appeal of cover illustrations and headlines, or does the appeal appear to be seasonally consistent and based on such features as holiday decorating or meal planning?

- Look at the pricing of the publication. Have the cover price and promotion remained consistent? Have competitors changed their pricing or promotion?

- Look at the state of the national economy. Are there external influences that may change patterns?

- After studying the above considerations, make a "judgmental" projection of the percentage change in circulation, then multiply that percentage times the average circulation.

In the example above, will the June issue next year be 31% above the current year's average circulation? The only holiday in June is Father's Day, so a projection of 100% (no change) is probably more realistic.

100% (Projected June Percentage) × 4,652,022 Average Circulation
= 4,652,022 Estimated June Circulation

**Chapter 13
Review Problems**

The following table reports television viewing in Atlanta.

Monday-Friday 8 P.M.–11 P.M., Men 25–54							
Persons Viewing TV				Indices			
NOV	FEB	MAY	JUL	NOV	FEB	MAY	JUL
49	52	46	41	100	106	94	84

1. What does the May index of 94 mean?

   _____

   _____

   _____

2. What adjustment factor should be applied to the ratings (men 25-54) for an Atlanta *July* prime time TV schedule bought and rated on the *February* rating book?

   _____

3. What adjustment factor should be applied to the ratings (men 25-54) for an Atlanta *February* prime time TV schedule bought and rate on the *November* rating book?

   _____

4. An Atlanta prime time television schedule of 600 GRPs (men 25-54) based on February ratings will typically deliver how many seasonally adjusted rating points in July?

   _____

5. A specific program in Atlanta is reported in the May rating book to have a 12 rating (27 share) for men 18 +. The same program is expected to grow to a 32 share in November. Persons viewing television (PVT) also changes from May to November. For the time period Tuesday 8:00-8:30 p.m. the May PVT is 44 for men 18 +, and it is likely to be 47 PVT in November based on the prior November rating book.

   What is the estimated rating for the program in November? Show how the rating is calculated.

   _____

   _____

6. If a publication has a circulation of 6,500,000 and a growth pattern that suggest an annual percentage change of 110%, what is the projected circulation for next year?

_____

_____

14 Cognitive Analysis:
The importance of thought in interpreting qualitative data

The single greatest danger in systematizing and formalizing a complex process such as media analysis is the temptation to replace thought with formula. The purpose of this chapter is to demonstrate the absolute necessity for insightful thinking while quantifying qualitative factors to be considered in a media analysis. A secondary purpose is to explain the methods which can be used in assigning values to qualitative measurements.

Paramount in all media planning is the consideration of qualitative values of media as they might affect communication of the specific product and message to be advertised. Qualitative values may be applied to all media and are not exclusive to magazine analysis. However, the depth and breadth of factors considered in print analysis make it well suited to demonstrate the concepts and applications proposed in cognitive analysis. In print analysis, for example, one or more of the following qualitative factors may be considered:

Editorial environment/compatibility

- Percent of editorial devoted to food, travel, decorating, etc.
- Specific editorial content (for example, recipes, west coast travel ideas, wallpaper use ideas)
- Perceived superiority in graphics or editorial
- Past experience regarding ad/edit positioning

Competitive environment

- Advertising to edit ratio
- Number of competitive advertising pages
- Promised separation from competitive ads
- Past experience regarding ads backed with another advertiser's coupon or adjacent to other ads

Advertising reproduction quality

- Consistency throughout the press run
- Quality control in regional or demographic editions
- Color match, balance, consistency, and registration
- Past experience regarding adjustment for misprints

Perceived reader involvement/confidence

- Circulation/audience trend and forecast
- Percent renewal of subscriptions; number of copies sold at full rate (subscription and newsstand); cover price/subscription cost
- Page-openings by reader and time spent reading
- Past experience of reader involvement or responsiveness, for example, coupon redemption, recipe or reprint requests

Characteristic of qualitative factors is the lack of uniformity in measurement base. One factor may be measured in percentages, a second factor measured in number of pages, and still other factors measured on a judgmental scale. Consequently, it is usually necessary to convert qualitative data to a simple and uniform value scale, such as a 5-point or 10-point scale. If the method of conversion to a scale is performed properly, the scores of various qualitative measurements can be combined (added or averaged) without distortion or bias.

There are four methods preferred for assigning values to qualitative measurements, and the method selected can have significant influence on the discriminating capacity of the measurement. Choice of the wrong method can overlook differences that should be considered. Therefore, application of a quantification process is no excuse for lack of perceptive thought or considered selection of method. All four methods have preference over an eyeball assignment of scores based on natural groupings. The four methods are summarized below and then explained in detail.

Assigning Values to Qualitative Data

Method 1: Select the highest measurement value and give it the highest score (for example, a 5 on a 5-point scale).

Method 2: Find the mean (arithmetic average) and give it the mean score (for example, a 3 on a 5-point scale).

Method 3: Find the median (place measurement values in rank order and find the middle value counting in from each end). Give the median the mean score (for example, a 3 on a 5-point scale).

Method 4: Find the mode (the measurement value that occurs most frequently). Give the mode the mean score (for example, a 3 on a 5-point scale).

We must begin any discussion of assigning values by discouraging an *eyeball* technique. It is the simplest, and consequently, most widely used technique. However, the method is not one of the four preferred methods because it permits disproportionate biasing of the value scores.

Example:

Magazine	% Edit Devoted to Decorating/Furnishing*	Assigned Score Eyeball Method
Deco Home	36.0%	5
Home A	34.8	5
Home B	30.3	5
Home C	15.0	4

Magazine	% Edit Devoted to Decorating/Furnishing*	Assigned Score Eyeball Method
Women A	6.6	3
Women B	6.2	3
Women C	5.5	3
Regn'l Home	3.2	2
Women D	2.9	2
Women E	2.9	2
Women F	2.4	2

*Source: a syndicated editorial measurement service.

Note that the value difference between the scores is not proportional to the difference in the specific measurements, for example, *Home B* has twice the share of compatible editorial than does *Home C* (30.3 vs 15.0), but it has only a 25% score advantage (5 vs 4). *Women F* has 16% of the *Home C* share of compatible editorial (2.4 ÷ 15.0), but it has 50% of *Home C's* score (2 ÷ 4).

The bias of the eyeball technique is compounded when scores for multiple qualitative factors are combined. For example:

Magazine	% Compatible Edit %	Score	# Wallpaper Use Ideas #	Score	Combined Score
Deco Home	36%	5	10	4	9
Home C	15%	4	11	5	9

Note that a major difference in editorial compatibility might be neutralized by only a slight difference in the second qualitative factor.

Method 1: Highest value receives maximum score.

This measurement assures that at least one vehicle will get the maximum score (for example, a 5 on a 5-point scale). It focuses discrimination among the top vehicles.

Procedure:

1. Select the highest measurement value as a base.
2. Divide all measurements by that base to obtain an index.*
3. Multiply the index of each vehicle by the maximum value on the selected scale (for example, a 5 on a 5-point scale).

Example:

Magazine	% Compatible Editorial	Index (36.0 = 100)*	Score (100 = 5)
Deco Home	36.0%	100	5.0
Home A	34.8	97	4.9
Home B	30.3	84	4.2
Home C	15.0	42	2.1
Women A	6.6	18	.9
Women B	6.2	17	.8
Women C	5.5	15	.8
Regn'l Home	3.2	9	.5
Women D	2.9	8	.4
Women E	2.9	8	.4
Women F	2.4	7	.3

Note that this example allows little distinction or value for the last seven magazines (six women's magazines and *Regn'l Home*).

Method 1 is most often used when the selected qualitative factor (for example compatible editorial) is intended to be a major determinant in the vehicle selection. The vehicles with a high score receive distinct advantage, and those with low scores receive minor attention.

*Footnote: The step of finding the index in Method 1 is shown for consistency with the other methods. However, an alternative mathematical process produces the same results, as follows:

1. Divide the highest measurement value by the maximum value on the selected measurement scale, thus determining an adjustment factor (for example, $36.0 \div 5.0 = 7.2$).
2. Divide the measurement value of each vehicle by the adjustment factor to obtain the score (for example, *Women A*: $6.6 \div 7.2 = 0.9$).

Method 2: Mean value receives the mean score.

This method assures that the average vehicle receives the average score. The focus of discrimination is directed to the average vehicles.

Procedures:

1. Determine the mean (arithmetic average) of the measurement values.
2. Divide all measurements by that average value (base) to obtain an index.
3. Multiply the index of each vehicle by the mean value (average value) on the selected scale (for example, a 3 on a 5-point scale).
4. Round all values in excess of the maximum so that none exceed the upper limits of the scale (for example, none exceeding a 5 on a 5-point scale).

Example:

Magazine	% Compat. Edit.	Index (Av=100)	Score (100=3)
Deco Home	36.0%	271	8.1 = 5
Home A	34.8%	262	7.9 = 5
Home B	30.3%	228	6.8 = 5
Home C	15.0%	113	3.4
Women A	6.6%	50	1.5
Women B	6.2%	47	1.4
Women C	5.5%	41	1.2
Regn'l Home	3.2%	24	.7
Women D	2.9%	22	.7
Women E	2.9%	22	.7
Women F	2.4%	18	.5
Average	145.8 ÷ 11 = 13.3	100	3.0

Note that the example now shows more distinction between publications having less than a 5 score, but no distinction between the top three publications. (The 20% advantage of *Deco Home* over *Home B* is eliminated.)

Method 2 is most often used when the major contenders fall in the average range of value. Extremely low scoring vehicles are likely to drop from contention, and high-scoring vehicles tend to be a small, selective group whose lead in the qualitative measurement does not warrant proportional advantage in the scoring.

Method 3: Median value receives the mean score.

This method prevents the extreme values on either end from influencing the score. Focus of discrimination is directed at the center or middle values.

Procedures:

1. List the measurement values in rank order.
2. Determine the median (the middle value counting in from each end of the measurements listed in rank order). There should be just as many numbers above the median as there are below the median. When a set of numbers contains an even number of members, there is no middle number. In this case, give the mean (average) of the two middle numbers as the median.
3. Divide all measurements by that middle value (base) to obtain an index.
4. Multiply the index of each vehicle by the median value (or mean value) on the selected scale (for example, a 3, on a 5-point scale).
5. Round all values in excess of the maximum so that none exceed the upper limits of the scale (for example, none exceed 5 on a 5-point scale).

Example:

Magazine	% Compat. Edit.	Index (6.2=100)	Score (100=3)
Deco Home	36.0%	581	17.4 = 5
Home A	34.8%	561	16.8 = 5
Home B	30.3%	489	14.7 = 5
Home C	15.0%	242	7.3 = 5
Women A	6.6%	106	3.2
Women B	6.2% (Median)	100	3.0
Women C	5.5%	89	2.7
Regn'l Home	3.2%	52	1.6
Women D	2.9%	47	1.4
Women E	2.9%	47	1.4
Women F	2.4%	39	1.2

Note that the example provides even less distinction among the top-rated publications. (There is no recognition of *Home B's* 100% editorial advantage over *Home C*).

Method 3 is most often used when there are vehicles with extremely low and high scores while the major contenders fall somewhere in between. The low-scoring vehicles are likely to drop from contention, and the high-scoring vehicles have a lead in qualitative measurement in excess of what should be proportionally reflected in the assigned score. In the above example, any magazine with greater than 15% compatible editorial is judged to have the same degree of advantage (that is, a 5 score).

Method 4: Mode value receives the mean score.

This method eliminates extreme values and least common values from influencing the score. Focus of discrimination is directed at the most frequently occurring value.

Procedure:

1. List the measurement values in rank order.
2. Identify the values which occur two or more times.
   The number that occurs most frequently in a set of numbers is called the *mode*.

   - If no number occurs more than once, the mode does not exist (there is no mode).

   - If two or more numbers occur the same number of times, there can be more than one mode for the set of numbers. When two numbers occur with the same frequency and occur more often than any other number, the set of numbers is bi-modal.

3. Divide all measurements by the mode value (base) to obtain an index.

   - If no mode is present, there is neither a basis nor reason for using this method for interpreting the data.

   - If more than one mode exists, choose one mode as the base. The mode of highest value is usually chosen so that the major focus of discrimination is directed to the values of greatest importance.

4. Multiply the index of each vehicle by the mean value (average) on the selected scale (for example, a 3 on a 5-point scale).
5. Round all values in excess of the maximum so that none exceed the upper limits of the scale (for example, none exceed 5 on a 5-point scale).

Example:

Magazine	% Compat. Edit.	Index (6.2=100)	Score (100=3)
Deco Home	36.0%	1241	37.2 = 5
Home A	34.8%	1200	36.0 = 5
Home B	30.3%	1045	31.4 = 5
Home C	15.3%	528	15.8 = 5
Women A	6.6%	228	6.8 = 5
Women B	6.2%	214	6.4 = 5
Women C	5.5%	190	5.7 = 5
Regn'l Home	3.2%	110	3.3
Women D	2.9% ⎤ (Mode)	100	3.0
Women E	2.9% ⎦	100	3.0
Women F	2.4%	83	2.5

Note that in this example the mode appeared in the low end of the listing. However, the mode may appear anywhere in a listing because it simply is the most frequently appearing value or concentration of values. Values outside the mode cluster tend to have minor discrimination as exemplified in the top seven vehicles all scoring 5.

Method 4 is most often used when there is similarity of value among major contenders, and the desire is to discriminate between these contenders without distraction or dilution of differences caused by the diverse array of the other vehicles.

Summary:

Qualitative values are important considerations in media analysis, and care must be applied in the selection of these values.

Equally important are the interpretation and utilization of these qualitative measurements. Careful thought must be applied to the method selected to quantify the qualitative measurements for use in the analysis process. The choice of method can focus on the various characteristics of the data and can have significant influence on the discriminating capacity of the data.

Method 1 The highest value receives the maximum score.
This method focuses discrimination among the top vehicles.

Method 2 The mean value receives the mean score.
This method focuses discrimination among the average vehicles.

Method 3 The median value receives the mean score.
This method eliminates extremes and focuses discrimination among the center or middle values.

Method 4 The mode value receives the mean score.
This method eliminates extremes and focuses discrimination among the most common values.

Eyeball or arbitrary methods of assigning a scale should be avoided.

Following is a composite chart showing the different methods of determining qualitative scores as they affect the example.

Methods of Converting Data to a Scale
Summary of Examples

Magazine	% Compatible Editorial	Eyeball by Cluster (Disproportionate)	Method 1 Highest Score	Method 2 Mean Value	Method 3 Median Value	Method 4 Mode Value
Deco Home	36.0%	5	5.0	5.0	5.0	5.0
Home A	34.8	5	4.9	5.0	5.0	5.0
Home B	30.3	5	4.2	5.0	5.0	5.0
Home C	15.0	4	2.1	3.4	5.0	5.0
Women A	6.6	3	0.9	1.5	3.2	5.0
Women B	6.2	3	0.8	1.4	3.0	5.0
Women C	5.5	3	0.8	1.2	2.7	5.0
Regn'l Home	3.2	2	0.5	0.7	1.6	3.3
Women D	2.9	2	0.4	0.7	1.4	3.0
Women E	2.9	2	0.4	0.7	1.4	3.0
Women F	2.4	2	0.3	0.5	1.2	2.5

Chapter 14 Review Problems

1. Match the method of assigning a value scale (Method 1, 2, 3, or 4) with the method's characteristic focus of discrimination (Characteristic A, B, C, or D).

Method 1 The highest value receives maximum score
Characteristic _____.

Method 2 The mean value receives mean score
Characteristic _____.

Method 3 The median value receives mean score
Characteristic _____.

Method 4 The mode value receives mean score
Characteristic _____.

Characteristic A: Eliminates extremes and focuses discrimination among the center or middle values.
Characteristic B: Eliminates extremes and focuses discrimination among the most common values.
Characteristic C: Focuses discrimination among the top vehicles.
Characteristic D: Focuses discrimination among the average vehicles.

2. Assign a value, based on a 5-point scale, using methods 1, 2, 3, and 4 for each of six advertising vehicles.

Medium	Qualitative Measurement	Method for Assigning Value Scores 1	2	3	4
A	124	_____	_____	_____	_____
B	92	_____	_____	_____	_____
C	92	_____	_____	_____	_____
D	78	_____	_____	_____	_____
E	29	_____	_____	_____	_____
F	28	_____	_____	_____	_____
G	25	_____	_____	_____	_____
H	23	_____	_____	_____	_____
I	14	_____	_____	_____	_____
J	5	_____	_____	_____	_____

Proficiency Tests

Following are two self-administered tests (Test A and Test B). Either test should reveal areas of media math needing further study and practice by the examinee.

The tests are not timed, but hesitancy and uncertainty should be sufficient encouragement to prompt review of the explanation and example section of the manual.

The second test permits re-testing and extended practice. The two tests differ in specific numbers, but not in mathematical procedures.

A necessary tool for rapid solution of media calculations is a calculator. Full utilization of your calculator is expected for completion of the tests.

The test answer sheet shows the mathematical process followed, the answer, and the functions of your calculator that should have been utilized.

You may wish to record your answers on a separate sheet of paper so that the test is clean for subsequent use and review.

Proficiency Test A

1. Calculator Skills

   Complete the following calculations, rounding answers to the nearest hundredth.

   a. $\begin{array}{r} 394.123 \\ +287.321 \\ \hline \end{array}$ b. $\begin{array}{r} 394.123 \\ -287.321 \\ \hline \end{array}$

   c. $394.1 \div 287.3 =$ d. $\begin{array}{l} 61 \quad\ \times 57 = \\ 47 \quad\ \times 57 = \\ 35.6 \quad \times 57 = \\ 28.123 \times 57 = \underline{} \\ \text{Total (Sum)} = \end{array}$

   e. $\begin{array}{r} 372 \div 14 = \\ 91 \div 14 = \\ 112 \div 14 = \\ 149 \div 14 = \underline{} \\ \text{Total (Sum)} \quad = \end{array}$

   f. $(794 - 227) \times 6 \times 4 = \underline{} - 314 = \underline{}$

2. Percentages

   a. Change the percents to decimals.

   $30\% = \underline{}$

   $22.5\% = \underline{}$

   $115\% = \underline{}$

   $6.2\% = \underline{}$

b. Change the decimals to percents.

.75 = _____

.372 = _____

1.04 = _____

.103 = _____

c. Change the common fractions to percents, rounding to the nearest tenth percent.

4/5 = _____

3/7 = _____

8/3 = _____

1/12 = _____

d. Calculate the following percentages, rounding to the nearest tenth.

45% of 365 = _____

15.5% of 28 = _____

175% of 32 = _____

27 is _____% of 36

14 is _____% of 57

38 is _____% of 25

e. Determine the percentage each quarter's billing represents of the total year's billing. Round to the nearest tenth percent.

First quarter $1,755,774   _____

Second quarter   2,175,209   _____

Third quarter   2,817,634   _____

Fourth quarter   3,005,683   _____

f. 1985's budget of $7,350,000 is 84% of the 1986 budget. What is the 1986 budget?

g. The net cost of an ad in a weekly newspaper is $750.00. What is the gross cost?

h. The gross cost of a magazine insertion is $69,600, less a special section discount of 20%. What is the discounted gross cost? What is the agency commission?

3. Indexing

a. Index the annual advertising expenditure of competitive brands compared to Brand X.

	Advertising Expenditures	Index
Brand X	$12,175,300	_____
Competitive Brand A	9,168,500	_____
Competitive Brand B	11,566,600	_____
Competitive Brand C	14,000,000	_____
Competitive Brand D	8,157,700	_____

b. Index the circulation of the women's magazine to the base year of 1980.

Year	Circulation	Index
1975	6,409,000	_____
1976	6,653,000	_____
1977	7,201,000	_____
1978	7,492,000	_____
1979	7,913,000	_____
1980	7,368,000	_____
1981	7,407,000	_____
1982	7,987,000	_____
1983	7,878,000	_____
1984	8,059,000	_____
1985	8,094,000	_____

4. Product Usage Index
   a. A specific product is primarily used by adult males (70% of its users). Men comprise 48% of the U.S. population. What is the product usage index for males?

   _____

   b. Calculate the index for widget product usage for each of the following three age segments.

Demographic Segment	Total U.S. Population (%)	Widget Users (%)	Index
18-34	39.7	36.2	_____
35-54	31.7	40.7	_____
55 or over	28.6	23.1	_____

5. Geographic Index
   a. The South Atlantic states account for 19% of a product's sales and only 16% of the U.S. population. Would the region's sales index be above or below 100? What is the index?

   Above _____ or Below _____ Index _____

   b. If Washington DC represents 4% of a brand's sales, 2% of the product category sales, and 2% of the U.S. population, what are the market's BDI and CDI?

   BDI _____ CDI _____

6. Averages

   For each of the following sets of numbers, determine the mean, median, and mode. Then select which of these three averages is most typical of the set of numbers.

   a. 957
      93
      82
      91
      87
      82
      84

      mean _____

      median _____

      mode _____

      most typical _____

   b. 2.1
      13.7
      8.0
      10.5
      7.3
      11.6
      9.4
      9.4

      mean _____

      median _____

      mode _____

      most typical _____

7. Weighting

Given the audience size and value weights shown below, calculate the weighted audience for each television package.

Demographic	Assigned Value Weight	Unweighted Audience (000)	
		Package A	Package B
Males 18-24	50	48,500	54,800
Males 25-54	100	182,900	180,700
Males 55+	25	81,100	78,200
Females 18+	−0−	281,000	275,000
Total		593,500	588,700

8. CPM

a. Given the weighted target audience and costs for three magazine schedules, determine the cost per thousand for each schedule.

Magazine Mix	Weighted Audience	Cost
Schedule A	213,832,700	$2,198,200
Schedule B	222,477,300	2,174,300
Schedule C	226,796,000	2,272,500

b. Network daytime television for a particular period is anticipated to cost $3100 per point (CPP) for women 25-54 years of age. There are 45,470,000 women 25-54 in United States TV households. What is the CPM for a schedule of 400 TRPs?

c. A spot radio market is expected to have a CPM of $6.60 among men 25-54 years of age in the TSA. Given the TSA population of men 25-54 is 1,668,800, calculate the anticipated cost per point (rounded to the nearest whole dollar).

9. Ratings, Shares, and HUTs

A specific episode of a program had an adult female audience of 14,812,000 out of a total of 86,350,000 women in television households.

    a. What was the program rating for adult women? Round to the nearest whole rating point.

    b. If the household rating was 22 and the HUTs were 72, what was the program's approximate share of viewing?

10. GRPs, Reach, and Frequency

The four-week schedule listed below reached 76% of men 25-54 years of age.

Program	Rating Men 25-54	Number of Units in 4-Week Period
Program A	16	3
Program B	19	2
Program C	14	3
Program D	18	4

    a. What are the total GRPs for the four weeks?

    b. What is the four-week average frequency of exposure among men 25-54 years of age?

11. Frequency Distribution and Effective Frequency
Following is the frequency distribution for a television schedule that delivers a reach of 72% and an average frequency of 4.0.

Frequency Distribution	
# Exposures	Reach
1+	72%
2+	61%
3+	54%
4+	41%
5+	23%
6+	15%
7+	11%

a. What is the estimated reach that can be achieved with a frequency of three or more times?

_____

b. If marketing considerations and experience suggest that four or more exposures are needed to be "effective," what is the estimated reach at this effective frequency?

_____

12. Media Forecasting
The following table reports television viewing in Atlanta.

Monday-Friday 7 P.M.–10 P.M., Men 25–54							
Persons Viewing TV				Indices			
NOV	FEB	MAY	JUL	NOV	FEB	MAY	JUL
49	52	46	41	100	106	94	84

a. What adjustment factor should be applied to the ratings (men 25-54) for an Atlanta *May* prime time TV schedule bought and rated on the *February* rating book?

_____

b. An Atlanta prime time television schedule of 500 GRPs (men 25-54) based on February ratings will typically deliver how many seasonally adjusted rating points in July?

_____

Media Math Proficiency Test A

Answer Sheet

1. Calculator Skills

   Calculator setting:
   5/4 rounding
   2 decimal places (round to nearest hundredth)

   a. 394.123
       +287.321
       ─────────
       681.44−

   b. 394.123
       −287.321
       ─────────
       106.80−

   c. $394.1 \div 287.3 = 1.37$

   d. Calculator functions:
      Multiplication by a constant and accumulate totals in memory

61	$\times$ 57 =	3,477.00
47	$\times$ 57 =	2,679.00
35.6	$\times$ 57 =	2,029.20
28.123	$\times$ 57 =	1,603.01
Total (Sum)	=	9,788.21

   e. Calculator functions:
      Division by a constant and accumulate totals in memory

372	$\div$ 14 =	26.57
91	$\div$ 14 =	6.50
112	$\div$ 14 =	8.00
149	$\div$ 14 =	10.64
Total (Sum)	=	51.71

   f. Calculator functions:
      Chain calculations

      Although each step of the calculation is shown below, the use of the chain calculating capacity of your calculator should streamline the calculation and minimize use of the equals key.

$$794 - 227 = \quad 567$$
$$\underline{\times \quad 6}$$
$$3,402$$
$$\underline{\times \quad 4}$$
$$13,608$$
$$\underline{- \quad 314}$$
$$13,294$$

2. Percentages

a.
30% =	.30
22.5% =	.225
115% =	1.15
6.2% =	.062

b.
.75 =	75
.372 =	37.2%
1.04 =	104%
.103 =	10.3%

c. Calculator setting:
  5/4 rounding
  1 decimal place (assuming % key use)
Calculator function:
  Division using the % key

4/5 =	80 %
3/7 =	42.9%
8/3 =	266.7%
1/12 =	8.3%

d. Calculator setting:
  5/4 rounding
  1 decimal place (assuming % key use)
Calculator function:
  Multiplication and division using the % key

45% × 365 =	164.3
15.5% × 28 =	4.3
175% × 32 =	56.0

27 ÷ 36 =	75%
14 ÷ 57 =	24.6%
38 ÷ 25 =	152%

e. Calculator setting:
    5/4 rounding
    1 decimal place (assuming % key use)
  Calculator function:
    Division by a constant and use of the % key

First quarter	$1,755,774 ÷ 9,754,300 =	18.0%
Second quarter	2,175,209 ÷ 9,754,300 =	22.3%
Third quarter	2,817,634 ÷ 9,754,300 =	28.9%
Fourth quarter	3,005,683 ÷ 9,754,300 =	30.8%
		100.0%

f. Calculator setting:
    5/4 rounding
    0 decimal places (round to nearest dollar)
  Calculator function:
    Division by percent, using the % key

$$\$7,350,000 \quad\quad = 84\% \times n$$
$$\$7,350,000 \div 84\% = n$$
$$\$8,750,000 \quad\quad = n$$

g. Calculator setting:
    5/4 rounding
    2 decimal places (round to nearest cent)
  Calculator function:
    Division by percent, using % key, or multiply by 1.1765.
  Either answer is acceptable.

$$\$750 \quad\quad = 85\% \times n$$
$$\$750 \div 85\% = n$$
$$\$882.35 \quad\quad = n$$

or

$$\$750 \times 1.1765 = \$882.38$$

Note that the standard adjustment factor of 1.1765 is rounded to 4 decimal places, thus creating a 3 cent overstatement.

Calculator setting:
  5/4 rounding
  2 decimal places (round to nearest cent)
Calculator function:
  Multiplication using percents and chain calculations

$69,600 − (20% × 69,600) =   ?
$69,600 − $13,920   = $55,680
                            ×   15%
                          ─────────────
                          $ 8,352

or

$69,600 × 80%   = $55,680
                            ×   15%
                          ─────────────
                          $ 8,352

The discounted gross cost is $55,680.
The agency commission (15% of gross) is $8,352.

3. Indexing
   Calculator setting:
     5/4 rounding
     0 decimal places (round to the nearest whole number).
   Calculator function:
     Division by a constant, using % key.

a.

	Advertising Expenditure			Index
Brand X	12,175,300	÷	12,175,300	=	100
Competitive Brand A	9,168,500	÷	12,175,300	=	75
Competitive Brand B	11,566,600	÷	12,175,300	=	95
Competitive Brand C	14,000,000	÷	12,175,300	=	115
Competitive Brand D	8,157,700	÷	12,175,300	=	67

b.

Year	Circulation				Index
1975	6,409,000	÷	7,368,000	=	87
1976	6,653,000	÷	7,368,000	=	90
1977	7,201,000	÷	7,368,000	=	98
1978	7,492,000	÷	7,368,000	=	102
1979	7,913,000	÷	7,368,000	=	107
1980	7,368,000	÷	7,368,000	=	100
1981	7,407,000	÷	7,368,000	=	101
1982	7,987,000	÷	7,368,000	=	108
1983	7,878,000	÷	7,368,000	=	107
1984	8,059,000	÷	7,368,000	=	109
1985	8,094,000	÷	7,368,000	=	110

4. Product Usage Index
  a. Calculator setting
       5/4 rounding
       0 decimal places (round index to nearest whole number)
     Calculator function
       Chain calculation of multiplication followed by division:

$$\frac{70\% \text{ male users}}{48\% \text{ male population}} \times 100 = 146 \text{ index}$$

$$\frac{0.70}{0.48} \times 100 = 146 \text{ index}$$

  b. Calculator setting:
       5/4 rounding
       0 decimal places (round index to nearest whole number)
     Calculator function
       Chain calculation of multiplication followed by division:

$$(0.362 \times 100) \div .397 = 91 \text{ index}$$
$$(0.407 \times 100) \div .317 = 128 \text{ index}$$
$$(0.231 \times 100) \div .286 = 81 \text{ index}$$

5. Geographic Index

    a. *Above*   The U.S. population is the "norm" and is represented by 100 index. The sales percentage for the South Atlantic Region (19%) is larger than the region's share of the population (16%), so the index is also larger than ("above") 100.

    Calculator setting
      5/4 rounding
      0 decimal places (round index to nearest whole number)
    Calculator function
      Chain calculation of multiplication followed by division:

$$(0.19 \times 100) \div 0.16 = 119 \text{ index}$$

    b. Calculator setting
      5/4 rounding
      0 decimal places (round index to nearest whole number)
    Calculator function
      Chain calculation of multiplication followed by division:

$$\text{Washington DC BDI} = (0.04 \times 100) \div 0.02 = 200$$
$$\text{CDI} = (0.02 \times 100) \div 0.02 = 100$$

6. Averages

    a.

Mean	957
	93
	82
	91
	87
	82
	+ 84
	1,476 ÷ 7 = 211

The arithmetic mean is 211.

Median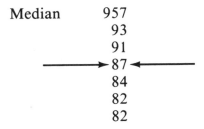

Place the numbers in descending (or ascending) order. The median is the number holding the middle position, the 4th from either end in this case. The median is 87.

Mode   957
93
91
87
84
82
82

82 is the mode because it occurs most frequently in this set of numbers.

The median, in this example, is the most typical average of the set of numbers. The extremely high number, 957, distorts the mean average, and the mode is clustered at the opposite extreme of the set.

b.

Mean   2.1
13.7
8.0
10.5
7.3
11.6
9.4
+ 9.4
————
72.0 ÷ 8 = 9.0

The arithmetic mean is 9.0.

Median 13.7

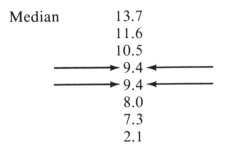

11.6

10.5

9.4

9.4

8.0

7.3

2.1

Place the numbers in descending (or ascending) order. The median is the number holding the middle position, in this case, the average of the two middle numbers. The median is 9.4.

Mode 13.7

11.6

10.5

9.4

9.4

8.0

7.3

2.1

9.4 is the mode because it occurs most frequently in this set of numbers.

In this example, the median and mode are identical and are the most typical average of the set of numbers.

7. Weighting

Calculator setting:
  5/4 rounding
  0 decimal places (round to the nearest whole number)
Calculator function:
  Multiplication using % key (weights are given as an index, and are therefore regarded as percentages). Accumulation of sum total in memory.

Demographic	Package A			Package B		
	Unweighted Audience	Weight	Weighted Audience	Unweighted Audience	Weight	Weighted Audience
	(000)		(000)	(000)		(000)
Males 18-24	48,500	× 50% =	24,250	54,800	× 50% =	27,400
Males 25-54	182,900	× 100% =	182,900	180,700	× 100% =	180,700
Males 55+	81,100	× 25% =	20,275	78,200	× 25% =	19,550
Females 18+	281,000	× −0− =	−0−	275,000	× −0− =	−0−
Total	593,500		227,425	588,700		227,650

8. CPM

a. Calculator setting:
5/4 rounding
2 decimal places (round to nearest cent)
Calculator function:
Simple division

Magazine Mix	Cost	Wt'd Audience ÷ 1000		CPM
Schedule A	$2,198,200	÷ 213,832.700	=	$10.28
Schedule B	2,174,300	÷ 222,477.300	=	9.77
Schedule C	2,272,500	÷ 226,796.000	=	10.02

b. Calculator setting:
5/4 rounding
2 decimal places (round to the nearest cent)
Calculator function:
Multiplication and division

$$CPM = (CPP \times 100) \div \frac{Population}{1,000}$$

$$CPM = (3100 \times 100) \div \frac{45,470,000}{1,000}$$

$$CPM = 310,000 \div 45,470$$

$$CPM = \$6.82$$

Alternative solution using TRPs:

$$CPM = (CPP \times TRPs) \div \frac{TRPs}{100} \times \frac{Population}{1,000}$$

$$CPM = (\$3100 \times 400) \div \frac{400}{100} \times \frac{45,470,000}{1,000}$$

$$CMP = \$1,240,000 \div (4 \times 45,470)$$

$$CPM = \$1,240,000 \div 181,880$$

$$CPM = \$6.82$$

c. Calculator setting:
   5/4 rounding
   0 decimal places (round to nearest whole dollar)
   Calculator function:
   Multiplication and division

$$CPP = CPM \times \frac{Population}{100,000}$$

$$CPP = \$6.60 \times \frac{1,668,800}{100,000}$$

$$CPP = \$6.60 \times 16.688$$

$$CPP = \$110$$

9. Ratings, Shares, and HUTs

   Calculator setting:
   5/4 rounding
   0 decimal places, assuming use of % key
   Calculator function:
   Division using % key

   a. Rating = Audience ÷ Population
      Rating = 14,812,000 ÷ 86,350,000
      Rating = 17 among women 18+ years of age (17% of all adult women in United States television households were viewing the program).

   b. Share = Rating (household) ÷ HUT
      Share = 22 ÷ 72
      Share = 31 (31% of those households viewing TV at that time were tuned to that program.)

10. GRPs, Reach, and Frequency

   a. Calculator setting:
       No special setting required
       Calculator function:
       Multiplication
       Accumulation of total sum in memory

Program	Rating Men 25-34		Number or Units in a 4-Week Period		GRPs
Program A	16	×	3	=	48
Program B	19	×	2	=	38
Program C	14	×	3	=	42
Program D	18	×	4	=	72
Total					200

   The schedule totals 200 GRPs among men 25-54.

   b. Calculator setting:
       5/4 rounding
       1 decimal place (round to nearest tenth)
       Calculator function:
       Division, chained to the previous calculation of total GRPs.

       Frequency (average week) = GRPs (4 week) ÷ Reach (4 week)
       Frequency   = 200   ÷ 76
       Frequency   = 2.6

11. Frequency Distribution and Effective Frequency
    a. 54%   b. 41%

12. Media Forecasting

  a. Calculator setting
    5/4 rounding
    1 decimal place (round to nearest tenth of a percent)
    Calculator function
    Chain calculation of multiplication followed by division:

$$\frac{46 \text{ PVT May}}{52 \text{ PVT Feb}} \times 100 = 88.5\% \text{ Adjustment Factor}$$

  b. *Step 1:* Calculator setting
      5/4 rounding
      1 decimal place (round to nearest tenth of a percent)
      Calculator function
      Chain calculation of multiplication followed by division:

$$\frac{\text{PVT, Men 25-54, 8-11 P.M., July}}{\text{PVT, Men 25-5, 8-11 P.M., Feb}} \times 100$$
$$= \text{Seasonal Adjustment Factor}$$

$$\frac{41 \text{ PVT July}}{52 \text{ PVT Feb}} \times 100 = 78.8\% \text{ Adjustment Factor}$$

  Step 2: Calculator setting
      5/4 rounding
      0 decimal places (round ratings to nearest whole number)
      Calculator function
      Multiplication

Feb to July Seasonal Adj. Factor × 500 GRPs (Feb. Ratings)
      = Estimated GRPs, July Delivery

78.8% Seasonal Adjustment Factor × 500 GRPs (Feb. Ratings)
      = 394 GRPs Estimated July Delivery

Proficiency Test B

1. Calculator Skills

   Complete the following calculations, rounding answers to the nearest hundredth.

   a. 513.264
       +327.234

   b. 486.321
       −295.107

   c. 873.2 ÷ 394.1 =

   d. 61   × 54 =
      47   × 54 =
      35.6   × 54 =
      28.123 × 54 = _____

      Total (Sum) =

   e. 372 ÷ 16 =
        91 ÷ 16 =
       112 ÷ 16 =
       149 ÷ 16 = _____

      Total (Sum) =

   f. (845 − 326) × 7 × 3 = _____ − 487 = _____

2. Percentages

   a. Change the percents to decimals.

      40% = _____

      31.7% = _____

      214% = _____

      9.6% = _____

b. Change the decimals to percents.

.81 = _____

.432 = _____

1.07 = _____

.359 = _____

c. Change the common fractions to percents, rounding to the nearest tenth percent.

3/4 = _____

7/8 = _____

9/7 = _____

5/14 = _____

d. Calculate the following percentages, rounding to the nearest tenth.

45% of 257 = _____

15.5% of 26 = _____

175% of 31 = _____

29 is __?__% of 36

12 is __?__% of 57

41 is __?__% of 23

e. Determine the percentage each quarter's billing represents of the total year's billing. Round to the nearest tenth percent.

First quarter	$1,755,902	_____
Second quarter	2,346,845	_____
Third quarter	2,904,331	_____
Fourth quarter	3,595,297	_____

f. 1985's budget of $7,350,000 is 80% of the 1986 budget. What is the 1986 budget?

g. The net cost of an ad in a weekly newspaper is $650.00. What is the gross cost?

h. The gross cost of a magazine insertion is $84,200, less a special section discount of 20%. What is the discounted gross cost? What is the agency commission?

3. Indexing

a. Index the annual advertising expenditure of competitive brands compared to Brand X.

	Advertising Expenditures	Index
Brand X	$12,375,300	_____
Competitive Brand A	9,168,500	_____
Competitive Brand B	11,566,600	_____
Competitive Brand C	14,000,000	_____
Competitive Brand D	8,157,700	_____

b. Index the circulation of the women's magazine to the base year of 1978.

Year	Circulation	Index
1975	6,409,000	_____
1976	6,653,000	_____
1977	7,201,000	_____
1978	7,492,000	_____
1979	7,913,000	_____
1980	7,368,000	_____
1981	7,407,000	_____
1982	7,987,000	_____
1983	7,878,000	_____
1984	8,059,000	_____
1985	8,094,000	_____

4. Product Usage Index
   a. A specific product is primarily used by adult females (80% of its users). Women comprise 52% of the U.S. population. What is the product usage index for females?

   _____

   b. Calculate the index for widget product usage for each of the following three age segments.

Demographic Segment	Total U.S. Population (%)	Widget Users (%)	Index
18-34	39.7	32.6	_____
35-54	31.7	42.1	_____
55 or over	28.6	25.3	_____

5. Geographic Index

   a. The South Atlantic states account for 21% of a product's sales and only 16% of the U.S. population. Would the region's sales index be above or below 100? What is the index?

   Above _____ or Below _____   Index _____

   b. If Detroit represents 3% of a brand's sales, 4% of the product category sales, and 2% of the U.S. population, what are the market's BDI and CDI?

   BDI _____   CDI _____

6. Averages

   For each of the following sets of numbers, determine the mean, median, and mode. Then select which of these three averages is most typical of the set of numbers.

   a. 921   mean _____
       93
       78   median _____
       91
       89   mode _____
       78
       77   most typical _____

   b. 2.6   mean _____
       16.2
       8.9   median _____
       11.7
       12.4   mode _____
       10.3
       7.6   most typical _____
       10.3

7. Weighting

Given the audience size and value weights shown below, calculate the weighted audience for each television package.

Demographic	Assigned Value Weight	Unweighted Audience (000) Package A	Package B
Males 18-24	50	51,200	60,300
Males 25-54	100	179,900	177,800
Males 55+	25	83,400	80,200
Females 18+	—0—	206,300	201,100
Total		520,800	519,400

8. CPM

a. Given the weighted target audience and costs for three magazine schedules, determine the cost per thousand for each schedule.

Magazine Mix	Weighted Audience	Cost
Schedule A	213,832,700	$2,385,200
Schedule B	222,477,300	2,164,300
Schedule C	226,796,000	2,501,700

b. Network daytime television for a particular period is anticipated to cost $3500 per point (CPP) for women 25-54 years of age. There are 45,470,000 women 25-54 in United States TV households. What is the CPM for a schedule of 400 TRPs?

c. A spot radio market is expected to have a CPM of $6.75 among men 25-54 years of age in the TSA. Given the TSA population of men 25-54 is 1,668,800, calculate the anticipated cost per point, rounded to the nearest whole dollar.

9. Ratings, Shares, and HUTs

A specific episode of a program had an adult female audience of 12,953,000 out of a total of 86,350,000 women living in TV households.

a. What was the program rating for adult women? Round to nearest whole rating point.

b. If the household rating was 20 and the HUTs were 72, what was the program's approximate share of viewing?

10. GRPs, Reach, and Frequency

The four-week schedule listed below reached 74% of men 25-54 years of age.

Program	Rating Men 25-54	Number of Units in 4-Week Period
Program A	17	3
Program B	19	3
Program C	15	2
Program D	18	4

a. What are the total GRPs for the four weeks?

b. What is the four-week average frequency of exposure among men 25-54 years of age?

11. Frequency Distribution and Effective Frequency
    Following is the frequency distribution for a television
    schedule that delivers a reach of 72% and an average
    frequency of 4.0.

Frequency Distribution	
# Exposures	Reach
1+	72%
2+	61%
3+	54%
4+	41%
5+	23%
6+	15%
7+	11%

a. What is the estimated reach that can be achieved
   with a frequency of two or more times?

   _____

b. If marketing considerations and experience
   suggest that five or more exposures are needed to
   be "effective," what is the estimated reach at this
   effective frequency?

   _____

12. Media Forecasting
    The following table reports television viewing in Minneapolis.

Monday-Friday 7 P.M.–10 P.M., Men 25–54							
Persons Viewing TV				Indices			
NOV	FEB	MAY	JUL	NOV	FEB	MAY	JUL
36	38	31	26	100	106	86	72

a. What adjustment factor should be applied to the ratings
   (men 25-54) for a Minneapolis *May* prime time TV
   schedule bought and rated on the *February* rating book?

   _____

b. A Minneapolis prime time television schedule of 500
   GRPs (men 25-54) based on February ratings will
   typically deliver how many seasonally adjusted rating
   points in July?

   _____

Media Math Proficiency Test B

Answer Sheet

1. Calculator Skills

   Calculator setting:

   5/4 rounding
   2 decimal places (round to nearest hundredth)

   a. 513.264
      $+327.234$
      840.50−

   b. 486.321
      -295.107
      191.21−

   c. 873.2 ÷ 394.1 = 2.22

   d. Calculator functions.

   Multiplication by a constant and accumulate totals in memory

61	× 54 =	3,294.00
47	× 54 =	2,538.00
35.6	× 54 =	1,922.40
28.123	× 54 =	1,518.64
Total (Sum)	=	9,273.04

   e. Calculator functions:

   Division by a constant and accumulate totals in memory

372	÷ 16 =	23.25
91	÷ 16 =	5.69
112	÷ 16 =	7.00
149	÷ 16 =	9.31
Total (Sum)	=	45.25

   f. Calculator functions:

   Chain calculations

   Although each step of the calculation is shown below, the use of the chain calculating capacity of your calculator should streamline the calculation and minimize the use of the equals key.

$$
\begin{array}{r}
845 - 326 = \quad 519 \\
\times \quad\quad 7 \\
\hline
3{,}633 \\
\times \quad\quad 3 \\
\hline
10{,}899 \\
- \quad 487 \\
\hline
10{,}412
\end{array}
$$

2. Percentages

a.
40% = .40
31.7% = .317
214% = 2.14
9.6% = .096

b.
.81 =   81%
.432 = 43.2%
1.07 = 107%
.359 = 35.9%

c. Calculator setting:
   5/4 rounding
   1 decimal place (assuming % key use)
   Calculator function:
   Division using the % key

3/4 =   75%
7/8 = 87.5%
9/7 = 128.6%
5/14 =   35.7%

d. Calculator setting:
   5/4 rounding
   1 decimal place (assuming % key use)
   Calculator function:
   Multiplication and division using the % key

45% × 257 = 115.7
15.5% × 26 =   4.0
175% × 31 = 54.3

$$29 \div 36 = 80.6\%$$
$$12 \div 57 = 21.1\%$$
$$41 \div 23 = 178.3\%$$

e. Calculator setting:
   5/4 rounding
   1 decimal place (assuming % key use)
   Calculator function:
   Division by a constant and use of the % key

First quarter	$1,755,902 \div 10,602,375 =$	16.6%
Second quarter	$2,346,845 \div 10,602,375 =$	22.1%
Third quarter	$2,904,331 \div 10,602,375 =$	27.4%
Fourth quarter	$3,595,297 \div 10,602,375 =$	33.9%
		100.0%

f. Calculator setting:
   5/4 rounding
   0 decimal places (round to nearest dollar)
   Calculator function:
   Division by percent, using the % key

$$\$7,350,000 \qquad = 80\% \times n$$
$$\$7,350,000 \div 80\% = n$$
$$\$9,187,500 \qquad = n$$

g. Calculator setting:
   5/4 rounding
   2 decimal places (round to nearest cent)
   Calculator function:
   Division by percent, using % key, or multiply by 1.1765.
   Either answer is acceptable.

$$\$650 \qquad = 85\% \times n$$
$$\$650 \div 85\% = n$$
$$\$764.71 \qquad = n$$

or

$$\$650 \times 1.1765 = \$764.73$$

Note that the standard adjustment factor of 1.1765 is rounded to 4 decimal places, creating a 2 cent overstatement.

h. Calculator setting:
   5/4 rounding
   2 decimal places (round to nearest cent)
   Calculator function:
   Multiplication using percents and chain calculations

$84,200 − (20% × 84,200) =   ?
$84,200 − $16,840   = $67,360
                    $ ×   15%
                    $10,104

or

$84,200 × 80% = $67,360
                ×   15%
                $10,104

They discounted gross cost is $67,360.
The agency commission (15% of gross) is $10,104.

3. Indexing
   Calculator setting:
      5/4 rounding
      0 decimal places (round to the nearest whole number).
   Calculator function:
      Division by a constant, using % key.

a.

	Advertising Expenditure				Index
Brand X	12,375,300	÷	12,375,300	=	100
Competitive Brand A	9,168,500	÷	12,375,300	=	74
Competitive Brand B	11,566,600	÷	12,375,300	=	93
Competitive Brand C	14,000,000	÷	12,375,300	=	113
Competitive Brand D	8,157,700	÷	12,375,300	=	66

b.

Year	Circulation				Index
1975	6,409,000	÷	7,492,000	=	86
1976	6,653,000	÷	7,492,000	=	89
1977	7,201,000	÷	7,492,000	=	96
1978	7,492,000	÷	7,492,000	=	100
1979	7,913,000	÷	7,492,000	=	106
1980	7,368,000	÷	7,492,000	=	98
1981	7,407,000	÷	7,492,000	=	99
1982	7,987,000	÷	7,492,000	=	107
1983	7,878,000	÷	7,492,000	=	105
1984	8,059,000	÷	7,402,000	=	108
1985	8,094,000	÷	7,492,000	=	108

4. Product Usage Index
   a. Calculator setting
      5/4 rounding
      0 decimal place (round index to nearest whole number)
      Calculator function
      Chain calculation of multiplication followed by division:

$$\frac{80\% \text{ female users}}{52\% \text{ female population}} \times 100 = 154 \text{ index}$$

$$\frac{0.80}{0.52} \times 100 = 154 \text{ index}$$

   b. Calculator setting
      5/4 rounding
      0 decimal places (round index to nearest whole number)
      Calculator function
      Chain calculation of multiplication followed by division:

$(0.326 \times 100) \div .397 = 82$ index
$(0.421 \times 100) \div .317 = 133$ index
$(0.253 \times 100) \div .286 = 88$ index

5. Geographic Index
   a. *Above* The U.S. population is the "norm" and is represented by 100 index. The sales percentage for the South Atlantic Region (21%) is larger than the region's share of the population (16%), so the index is also larger than ("above") 100.

   Calculator setting
   5/4 rounding
   0 decimal places (round index to nearest whole number)
   Calculator function
   Chain calculation of multiplication followed by division:

   $$(0.21 \times 100) \div 0.16 = 131 \text{ index}$$

   b. Calculator setting
   5/4 rounding
   0 decimal place (round index to nearest whole number)
   Calculator function
   Chain calculation of multiplication followed by division:
   Detroit $BDI = (0.03 \times 100) \div 0.02 = 150$
   $CDI = (0.04 \times 100) \div 0.02 = 200$

6. Averages
   a.

   Mean
   ```
            921
             93
             78
             91
             89
             78
         +  77
         ─────
          1,427  ÷ 7 = 204
   ```

The arithmetic mean is 204.

Median   921
               93
               91
       ⟶ 89 ⟵
               78
               78
               77

Place the numbers in descending (or ascending) order. The median is the number holding the middle position, the 4th from either end in this case. The median is 89.

Mode   921
               93
               91
               89
               78
               78
               77

78 is the mode because it occurs most frequently in this set of numbers.

The median, in this example, is the most typical average of the set of numbers. The extremely high number, 921 distorts, the mean average, and the mode is clustered at the opposite extreme of the set.

b.

Mean   2.6
            16.2
             8.9
           11.7
           12.4
           10.3
            7.6
       +10.3
         80.0 ÷ 8 = 10.0

The arithmetic means is 10.0.

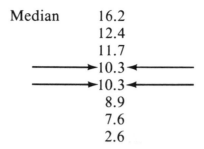

Median   16.2
            12.4
            11.7
            10.3
            10.3
             8.9
             7.6
             2.6

Place the numbers in descending (or ascending) order. The median is the number holding the middle position, in this case, the average of the two middle numbers. The median is 10.3.

Mode   16.2
            12.4
            11.7
            10.3
            10.3
             8.9
             7.6
             2.6

10.3 is the mode because it occurs most frequently in the set of numbers.

In this example, the median and mode are identical and are the most typical average of the set of numbers.

7. Weighting

Calculator setting:
    5/4 rounding
    0 decimal places (round to the nearest whole number)
Calculator function:
    Multiplication using % key (weights are given as an index, and are therefore regarded as percentages). Accumulation of sum total in memory.

Demographic	Package A			Package B		
	Unweighted Audience	Weight	Weighted Audience	Unweighted Audience	Weight	Weighted Audience
	(000)		(000)	(000)		(000)
Males 18-24	51,200	× 50% =	25,600	60,300	× 50% =	30,150
Males 25-54	179,900	× 100% =	179,900	177,800	× 100% =	177,800
Males 55+	83,400	× 25% =	20,850	80,200	× 25% =	20,050
Females 18+	206,300	× −0− =	−0−	201,100	× −0− =	−0−
Total	520,800		226,350	519,400		228,000

8. CPM

a. Calculator setting:
   5/4 rounding
   2 decimal places (round to nearest cent)
   Calculator function:
   Simple division

Magazine Mix	Cost		Wt'd Audience ÷ 1000		CPM
Schedule A	$2,385,200	÷	213,832.700	=	$11.15
Schedule B	2,164,300	÷	222,477.300	=	9.73
Schedule C	2,501,700	÷	226,796.000	=	11.03

b. Calculator setting:
   5/4 rounding
   2 decimal places (round to the nearest cent)
   Calculator function:
   Multiplication and division

$$\text{CPM} = (\text{CPP} \times 100) \div \frac{\text{Population}}{1,000}$$

$$\text{CPM} = (3500 \times 100) \div \frac{45,470,000}{1,000}$$

$$\text{CPM} = 350,000 \div 45,470$$

$$\text{CPM} = \$7.70$$

Alternative solution using TRPs:

$$\text{CPM} = (\text{CPP} \times \text{TRPs}) \div \frac{\text{TRPs}}{100} \times \frac{\text{Population}}{1,000}$$

$$\text{CPM} = (\$3500 \times 400) \div \frac{400}{100} \times \frac{45,470,000}{1,000}$$

$$\text{CMP} = \$1,400,000 \div (4 \times 45,470)$$

$$\text{CPM} = \$1,400,000 \div 181,880$$

$$\text{CPM} = \$7.70$$

c. Calculator setting:
   5/4 rounding
   0 decimal places (round to nearest whole dollar)
  Calculator function:
   Multiplication and division

$$\text{CPP} = \text{CPM} \times \frac{\text{Population}}{100,000}$$

$$\text{CPP} = \$6.75 \times \frac{1,668,800}{100,000}$$

$$\text{CPP} = \$6.75 \times 16.688$$

$$\text{CPP} = \$113$$

9. Ratings, Shares, and HUTs

   Calculator setting:
    5/4 rounding
    0 decimal places, assuming use of % key
   Calculator function:
    Division using % key

  a. Rating = Audience ÷ Population
     Rating = 12,953,000 ÷ 86,350,000
     Rating = 15 among women 18+ years of age (15% of all adult women in U.S. television households were viewing the program).

b. Share = Rating (household) ÷ HUT
   Share = 20   ÷ 72
   Share = 28 (28% of those households viewing TV at that time
          were tuned to that program.)

10. GRPs, Reach, and Frequency

a. Calculator setting:
   No special setting required
   Calculator function:
   Multiplication
   Accumulation of total sum in memory

Program	Rating Men 25-34		Number or Units in a 4-Week Period		GRPs
Program A	17	×	3	=	51
Program B	19	×	3	=	57
Program C	15	×	2	=	30
Program D	18	×	4	=	72
Total					210

The schedule totals 210 GRPs among men 25-54.

b. Calculator setting:
   5/4 rounding
   1 decimal place (round to nearest tenth)
   Calculator function:
   Division, chained to the previous calculation of total GRPs.

Frequency (average week) = GRPs (4 week) ÷ Reach (4 week)
Frequency   = 210   ÷ 74
Frequency   = 2.8

11. Frequency Distribution and Effective Frequency
    a. 61%   b. 23%

12. Media Forecasting
  a. Calculator setting
        5/4 rounding
        1 decimal place (round to nearest tenth of a percent)
     Calculator function
        Chain calculation of multiplication followed by division:

$$\frac{31 \text{ PVT May}}{38 \text{ PVT Feb}} \times 100 = 81.6\% \text{ Adjustment Factor}$$

  b. *Step 1:* Calculator setting
        5/4 rounding
        1 decimal place (round to nearest tenth of a percent)
     Calculator function
        Chain calculation of multiplication followed by division:

$$\frac{\text{PVT, Men 25-54, 8-11 P.M., July}}{\text{PVT, Men 25-54, 8-11 P.M., Feb}} \times 100$$

$$= \text{Seasonal Adjustment Factor (\%)}$$

$$\frac{26 \text{ PVT July}}{38 \text{ PVT Feb}} \times 100 = 68.4\% \text{ Adjustment Factor}$$

  Step 2: Calculator setting
        5/4 rounding
        0 decimal places (round ratings to nearest whole number)
     Calculator function
        Multiplication

Feb to July Seasonal Adj. Factor × 500 GRPs
        (Feb. Ratings) = Estimated GRPs, July Delivery

68.4% Seasonal Adjustment Factor × 500 GRPs
        (Feb. Ratings) = 342 GRPs Estimated July Delivery

Answers to Chapter Review Problems

Chapter 1	1. A. 1,771.571	2. A. 13.965
	B. 711	B. 102.001
	C. 315.243	C. 39.280
	D. 226.153	D. 139.313
	3. A. 972	4. A. 20.431
	B. 52.360	B. 15.945
	C. 340.607	C. 55.027
	D. 11,707.959	D. 306.395
	5. A. 54	5. B. 1.917
	135	1.167
	108	6.667
	423	3.167
	5. C. 591.7	5. D. 94.809
	29.1	693.238
	80.51	14.703
	350.17	70.98
	4.85	861.9

5. E. 38.148

     36.148

      7.370

     30.741

5. F. $ 35.404

     $ 89.577

     $ 61.865

     $155.808

6. A. 31

  B. 32

  C. 285.895

  D. $654.553

  E. $2,548.571

7. A. 35

    60

  1030

   745

   305

 2175

  725

7. B. 301.76

  1041.81

  1020.50

   407.88

 2,771.95

33,263.40

7. C. $47,619.25

  $32,982.42

  $31,582.42

  $50,697.08

  $35,975.50

$198,856.67

 $39,771.33

7. D. 69.668

  48.646

  87.055

  89.150

294.519

218.846

7. E.   448.0

         31.0

      370.8

       22.1

      <u>135.9</u>

   1,007.8

Chapter 2	1. A.	.05	1. F.	.038
	B.	.17	G.	.0136
	C.	.63	H.	.213
	D.	1.42	I.	2.9761
	E.	13.71	J.	40.025
	2. A.	6%	2. F.	3.2%
	B.	12%	G.	27.1%
	C.	391%	H.	100.9%
	D.	2,247%	I.	4,712.3%
	E.	.4%	J.	400%
	3. A.	60%	3. F.	60 %
	B.	87.5%	G.	63.64%
	C.	43.75%	H.	66.67%
	D.	3.13%	I.	214.29%
	E.	300%	J.	66.36%

4. A. 15.20   4. F. $ .77

   B. $15.20   G.   11.28

   C. 29.20   H.   43.20

   D. 65.00   I.   39.24

   E. 99.83   J. $35,166.20

5. A.   25%   5. F. 14.29%

   B. 33.33%   G. 31.11%

   C. 69.17%   H.   500%

   D. 59.25%   I.   50%

   E. 14.29%   J.   5.76%

6. A. Net A   10,480   31.3%

      Net B   12,650   37.7%

      Net C   10,390   31.0%

      Total   33,520   100.0%

6. B. Total Sales $3,659,813

January	5.7%	July	5.7%
February	7.8%	August	5.3%
March	8.6%	September	5.4%
April	12.8%	October	6.6%
May	12.5%	November	9.4%
June	8.8%	December	11.4%
		Total	100.0%

6. C. Total Expenditures. $5,958,900

        1st. Qtr.   21.0%

        2nd. Qtr.   23.8%

        3rd. Qtr.   15.3%

        4th. Qtr.   <u>39.9%</u>

        Total   100.0%

7.	A.	171.43		7.	F.	500.00
	B.	700.00			G.	600.00
	C.	900.00			H.	8,200.00
	D.	50.67			I.	$26,300.00
	E.	7,340.00			J.	$2,350,000

8. Program A   22,912 Male Viewers

   Program B   5,808

   Program C   4,875

   Program D   <u>18,054</u>

   Total   51,649

   % of Total Adult Viewers: 55%

Chapter 3

A.	85%	D.	$126,000
B.	$150	E.	$ 31,461
C.	$45,407	F.	$305,660 $53,940

G.	$478,338	$84,412		I.	$176,475	$26,475
					*($176,471	$26,471)*
H.	$588,250	$88,250				
	*($588,235	$88,235)*		J.	$ 47,060	$ 7,060
					*($ 47,059	$ 7,059)*

*Problems H, I, and J can be solved for gross by multiplying net times 1.1765, or by dividing the net by 85%. Multiplying by the factor 1.1765 is less precise mathematically, but is the more common method followed in advertising.

Chapter 4

1. A. 320

   B. 250

   C. 215

   D. 159

   E. 153

   F. 115

   G. 102

   H. 100

1. I. 89

   J. 62

   K. 59

   L. 57

   M. 50

   N. 44

   O. 43

2. A. 159

   B. 168

   C. 172

   D. 167

   E. 76

   F. 90

   G. 97

   H. 124

2. I. 99

   J. 68

   K. 45

   L. 70

   M. 46

   N. 58

   O. 59

3.	1975	86		1981	104
	1976	70		1982	98
	1977	80		1983	113
	1978	85		1984	120
	1979	91		1985	142
	1980	100			

4. 42%

5. 30%

Chapter 5

1. A. 137
   B. 66
   C. Women
   D. Men

2.

Demographic Segment	Index
18–24	83
25–34	96
35–44	130
45–54	126
55–64	104
65 or Over	62

3. Ages 35–54

4.

Demographic Segment	Index
Hshld Inc $50,000+	98
$40,000–49,999	116
$35,000–39,999	180
$25,000–34,999	104
$15,000–24,999	84
Less than $15,000	68

5. 100 Index (U.S. Population) − 15% = 85 index

6. 100 Index (U.S. Population) + 20% = 120 index

7. *D*, As much marketing information as is available.

Chapter 6

1.

TV Market	BDI	
New York	150	(11.4 ÷ 7.6)
Los Angeles–Palm Springs	120	(6.5 ÷ 5.4)
Chicago	78	(2.8 ÷ 3.6)
Boston	96	(2.2 ÷ 2.3)
Atlanta	200	(2.8 ÷ 1.4)

2.

TV Market	CDI	
New York	86	(6.5 ÷ 7.6)
Los Angeles–Palm Springs	119	(6.4 ÷ 5.4)
Chicago	131	(4.7 ÷ 3.6)
Boston	100	(2.3 ÷ 2.3)
Atlanta	143	(2.0 ÷ 1.4)

3. Atlanta. Atlanta represents only 2.8% of sales, while other markets have high BDI *and* considerably larger share of total sales. (For example, New York and Los Angeles.)

4. Chicago is facing difficulties (low BDI) that the category as a whole is not (high CDI). The market must be examined as to the cause of difficulties and the probability of improving the brand's position.

5. Los Angeles has excellent potential. Both brand and category have excellent sales opportunities. The brand's share of sales should probably be protected by continued support.

Chapter 7

		Mean	Median	Mode
1.	A.	66	71	54
	B.	48	55	29
	C.	580	571	None
	D.	7.07	8.06	3.7 & 9.1 Bi-Modal
	E.	832	828	784

2. $922,000 3. $4,067,400

4. Age: 39 Income: $26,800

5. $26,040

Chapter 8

1. A. 9,959
   B. 10,874
   C. 15,245

2. A. 31,088
   B. 30,666
   E. 22,286
   F. 23,528
   G. 19,975

1. D. 7,191
   E. 8,097
   F. 17,200

2. C. 23,249
   D. 22,018
   H. 11,914
   I. 16,671
   J. 11,965

3. **Index**

	Weighted Audience
A. 13	2,232
B. 53	9,448
C. 33	6,061
D. 20	2,480
E. 100	13,274
F. 67	11,524

4. Journal A: 100,280

Journal B: 95,200

Chapter 9

1. A. $10.79
   B. $11.12
   C. $14.88
   D. $11.56

1. E. $11.47
   F. $13.53
   G. $10.79

2. Magazine 4-C $4.20

    Magazine b/w $3.51

    Net TV Day $3.60

    Net TV Prime $10.25

    Net Radio $3.25

    Newspaper $12.50

    Outdoor $2.15

3. $4.06   4. $10.07

5. $5,020   6. $6,468

Chapter 10

1. A. 14.2   2. A. 1.9

   B. 11.7   B. 1.7

   C. 16.0   C. 1.6

   D. 19.1   D. 1.1

                            E. 1.0

3. A. 50   F. .9

   B. 12   G. .7

   C. 30   H. .5

   D. 55

   E. 30

   F. 26

Chapter 11

1. HH: 47.5

   W 18+ 39.1

   W 18-34 33.3

2. 431 GRP

3. 466 GRP

4. Smallest: 19%

   Largest 77%

5. Smallest: 9.1%

   Largest: 26.0%

6. A. 253

   B. 70%

   C. 7.1

   D. 60%

   E. 439

   F. 11.8

Chapter 12

1. 46%

2. 10%

3. 23%

4. 2 times = 13%
   3 times = 10%
   4 times = 8%
   5 times = 6%
   6 times = 4%
   Total   41% exposed 2-6 times

5. Commercial Wear Out

6. "Response Curve" or "Response Function"

7. Frequency distribution can clarify differences that may be obscured by "average frequency". It can demonstrate and compare presumed value at "effective frequency" levels.

Chapter 13

1. A prime time television schedule in Atlanta will typically deliver in May about 94% of the males 25 to 54 that the same schedule might deliver in November. November is the base month used for calculating the index because November shows a "100" index. Stated another way, 6% (100–94) fewer males 25–54 are likely to view a typical prime time schedule in May than in November in Atlanta.

2. $\dfrac{41 \text{ PVT July}}{52 \text{ PVT Feb}} \times 100 = 78.8\%$ Adjustment Factor

3. $\dfrac{52 \text{ PVT Feb}}{49 \text{ PVT Nov}} \times 100 = 106.1\%$ Adjustment Factor

   Or, referencing the index table which is calculated on a "base" of November, the adjustment factor is 106%.

4. *Step 1:* $\dfrac{\text{PVT, Men 25-54, 8-11 P.M., July}}{\text{PVT, Men 25-54, 8-11 P.M., Feb.}} \times 100$

   $= $ Seasonal Adjustment Factor (%)

   $\dfrac{41 \text{ PVT July}}{52 \text{ PVT Feb}} \times 100$

   $= 78.8\%$ Adjustment Factor

   Step 2: Feb to July Seasonal Adjustment Factor
   $\times 600$ GRPs (Feb. Ratings)

   $=$ Estimated GRPs, July Delivery

   78.8% Seasonal Adjustment Factor
   $\times 600$ GRPs (Feb. Ratings)

   $= 473$ GRPs Estimated July Delivery

5. Estimated November Share $\times$ PVT, Men 18+, Nov. for
   Tues. 8–8:30 P.M. $=$ Estimated Fall Rating

   $.32 \times 47 = 15$ Estimated November Rating

6. 110% Projected Change $\times$ 6,500,000 Current Circulation

   $= 7,150,000$ Estimated Circulation Next Year

Chapter 14
1. Method 1: C

   Method 2: D

   Method 3: A

   Method 4: B

2.

Medium	1	2	3	4
A	5.0	7.3 = 5.0	13.1 = 5.0	4.0
B	3.7	5.4 = 5.0	9.7 = 5.0	3.0
C	3.7	5.4 = 5.0	9.7 = 5.0	3.0
D	3.2	4.6	8.2 = 5.0	2.5
E	1.2	1.7	3.1	1.0
F	1.1	1.7	3.0	0.9
G	1.0	1.5	2.6	0.8
H	0.9	1.4	2.4	0.8
I	0.6	0.8	1.5	0.5
J	0.2	0.3	0.5	0.2

Method 1:   124 = 5.0

Method 2:   Mean is 51 and equal to 3.0

Method 3:   Median is 28.5 and equal to 3.0

Method 4:   Mode is 92 and equal to 3.0

Glossary/Index

ADI. See **Area of dominant influence.**

Agency commission. A percentage (usually 15%) of the cost of the advertising given by media to advertising agencies ordering the advertising (p. 27).

Algebraic logic. See **Calculator logic.**

Area of dominant influence (ADI). A geographic area defined by Arbitron, based on areas of primary television viewing (similar to Nielsen's designated market areas—DMAs) (p. 80).

Arithmetic average. See **Average—Mean.**

Arithmetic logic. See **Calculator logic.**

Average. A number that typifies a set of numbers or values. The average may be the mean, median, or mode (p. 55).

    Mean. The result of dividing the sum of a set of quantities by the number of quantities. Also called **arithmetic average** (p. 55).

    Median. The middle number in a series arranged in order of size (p. 57).

    Mode. The number which occurs most frequently in a set of numbers (p. 58).

BDI. See **Brand development index.**

Brand development index (BDI). An index that relates the percent of a brand's sales in a market to the percent of the U.S. population in that same market (p. 48).

Calculator logic. The system by which the calculator processes numerical input. There are two common logic systems, algebraic and arithmetic (p. 4).

Algebraic logic. Each number entered into the calculator is followed by a function key applying to the **next** number and concludes with an equal sign (p. 5).

Arithmetic logic. Each number entered into the calculator is followed by a function key applying to **that** number (p. 4).

Calculator skills.

Calculator logic	(p. 4)
Chain calculations	(p. 5)
Decimal selection	(p. 1)
Memory calculations	(p. 7)
Using a constant	(p. 3)

Category development index (CDI). An index that relates the percent of a product category's sales in a market to the percent of the U.S. population in that same market. (p. 48).

CDI. See **Category development index.**

Chain calculations. A sequence of calculations where each step utilizes the answer from the previous step (p. 5).

Constant. A number used in each of a series of similar multiplication or division calculations (p. 3).

Cost per rating point (CPP). The cost of a media vehicle (or media schedule) for reaching one rating point (one percent) of the specified audience (p. 73).

Cost per thousand (CPM). The cost of a media vehicle (or media schedule) for reaching each 1,000 of the specified audience (p. 71).

CPM. See **cost per thousand.**

CPP. See **cost per rating point.**

Cumulative audience (Cume). See **Reach.**

Decimal. A point punctuation which indicates that the numbers following the point are a fraction with an unwritten denominator of 10 or some power of ten (p. 1).

Changing decimals to percents (p. 14).

Mode key indicates if the last decimal is to be rounded (p. 2).

Rounding increases the last decimal shown in the calculator answer panel if the next digit has a value of 5 or more (p. 1).

Selector key indicates the number of decimal places showing in the answer panel of the calculator (p. 1).

Denominator. The number below or to the right of the line in a fraction. The denominator divides into the numerator (p. 14).

Designated market area (DMA). A geographic area defined by A.C. Nielsen, based on areas of primary television viewing. [Similar to Arbitron's **Area of dominant influence (ADI)**] (p. 80).

DMA. See **Designed market area.**

Effective frequency. A level or range of advertising frequency that is believed (based on judgment and/or experience) to accomplish the goals, such as stimulate response, change an attitude, or prompt a purchase (p. 93).

Efficiency. The relationship between circulation (or audience) and media cost, most commonly expressed as cost per thousand (p. 71).

Forecasting. Estimating or projecting future media performance (such as ratings or circulation) based on past media performance (p. 97).

Frequency. The number of times that the average household or person is exposed to the advertising among those reached at least once in a specific period of time (p. 88).

Frequency distribution. An array of incremental levels of advertising exposure. The array provides estimated reach at "cumulative" increments or "individual" increments of frequency. Examples of distribution at "cumulative" increments of frequency would be "those exposed one or more times to the advertising," "those exposed two or more times," "those exposed three or more times," etc. Examples of distribution at "individual" increments of frequency would be "those exposed only once to the advertising," "those exposed only twice," "those exposed only three times," etc. (p. 91).

Geographic indexing. See **Indexing geographic sales profile.**

Gross cost. The cost of media including agency commission (p. 27).

Gross rating points (GRPs). The sum of ratings achieved by a specific media vehicle or schedule (p. 85).

> **TRPs:** The sum of ratings of a specific demographic segment may be called **Target audience GRPs** or simply **TRPs** (p. 85).

Households using television (HUT). The percentage of all TV households in the survey area with one or more sets in use during a specific time period (p. 80).

Index. A mathematical expression relating one number to another (p. 33).

Indexing geographic sales profile. An index relating a product's geographic share of sales to the same geographic market's share of the U.S. population (p. 47). See also **BDI** and **CDI.**

Indexing product usage profile. An index relating a product's demographic characteristics to the same demographic characteristic's share of the U.S. population (p. 41).

Indexing sales. An index relating sales in a specific geographic market for a product (or product category) to the same geographic market's share of the U.S. population (p. 48). See also **BDI** and **CDI.**

Market indexing. See **Indexing geographic sales profile.**

Mean. See **Average.**

Media (singular, Medium). Communication vehicles, such as TV, radio, magazine, newspapers, and outdoor, particularly those accepting paid advertising.

Median. See **Average.**

Memory calculations. Using the memory functions of a calculator (p. 7).

Milline. An archaic form of CPM for newspapers. It is the cost of 1000 lines of advertising divided by the circulation in thousands (p. 76).

Mode. See **Average.**

Net cost. The cost of media after deducting the agency commission (p. 27).

Numerator. The number on top or to the left of the line in a fraction. The numerator is divided by the denominator (p. 14).

Percentage. A portion of an amount or number, expressed in hundredths followed by a percent sign (%) (p. 14).

    Changing decimals to percents   (p. 14).

    Changing fractions to percents   (p. 14).

    Changing percents to decimals   (p. 14).

    Percentaging using a constant   (p. 17).

Product usage index. See **Indexing product usage profile.**

Persons using television (PUT) and Persons viewing television (PVT). In common usage, both terms are interchangeable. A.C. Nielsen continues to use "PUT" and Arbitron changed to "PVT." The percentage of all persons (or of all persons in a demographic category) in the survey area who are viewing television during a specific period of time. (PUT or PVT as rating p. 80); (PUT or PVT in forecasting p. 98).

Rating. The audience of a particular TV or radio program or station at a particular time expressed as a percent of the audience population. The percent sign is not shown, and the rating may represent household viewing or a specific demographic audience segment's listening or viewing (p. 79).

Reach. The number or percent of different homes or persons exposed at least once to an advertising schedule over a specific period of time (p. 87). In broadcast, **reach** is also referred to as **cumulative audience (cume)** or net reach.

Renewal rate. The percentage of subscribers that renew their subscription, rather than let it lapse. Renewal is one indication of circulation vitality. (p. 67).

 Definitions

- 4C+
- Audience Composition
- Audience Skew
- Average Audience
- Cumulative Audience
- Is it possible to add Cumulative audience figures together?
- When buying or selling radio, is it better to use Averages or Cumes?
- Cost Efficiency
- Cost Per TARP or Cost Per Target Audience Rating Point
- Cost PerThousand (C.P.M.)
- Coverage
- Coverage Area
- Day Part
- Demographics
- Diary Method
- Effective Frequency
- Exclusive Audience
- FPC
- Frequency Distribution
- Gross Impacts
- Listeners
- Market Share
- Media Mix
- Post Analysis
- RadioScope
- Reach and Frequency
- Sample
- Sessions (Cumes and Averages)
- Share of Audience
- S.C.CM
- Socio/Economic Data
- Target Audience
- Time Spent Listening

4C+
4 Colour plus

Audience Composition
Is a general term describing the range and type of audience breakdowns or classifications available in media audience measurement surveys.

Audience Skew
Is a term describing the situation when the audience for a particular medium or media vehicle is distributed (by some stated audience composition breakdown) in a manner different to what might be described as "normal".

Example:
A particular radio station may attract the great proportion of the available teenage listeners. This audience would be described as "skewed" towards the younger age groups.

Average Audience
The term "Average Audience" refers to the estimated audience of a particular station over a stated period of time.*

For example, if a given station is reported with audiences over four consecutive quarter hours as 20,000, 22,000, 24,000 and 26,000 then the average audience for that station over that one hour time period is calculated as 23,000 listeners. As such, an average audience estimate will provide an advertiser with an approximation of what

audience may be exposed to one commercial placed at random within the given time period. However, caution must conceal significant fluctuations in audience within the time period. For example, a time period commencing at 5.30am and concluding at 9.00pm will most likely include the two extremes of audience listening levels throughout the week.

Cumulative Audience
Cumulative Audience is the number of different people reached at least once by a station over a given period of time, normally for at least 15 minutes.*

Another term used to express cumulative audience is 'Reach'.

The concepts of 'cumulative audience' and 'average audience' are better understood with reference to a bus journey. A particular vehicle may, over the course of one journey, carry a total of 350 different passengers for varying distances (this represents the 'cumulative audience' of the vehicle). However, in the course of the journey, the average load may well have been 20 people (or the 'average audience').

*as defined by AC Nielsen McNair

Is it possible to add Cumulative audience figures together?
Some cumulative figures may be added. For example, cumulative audience estimates for separate demographics or age groupings may be added together for a result for the larger, combined age group.

Other cumulative audience estimates may not be added. For example, for a given station, the cumulative audience for one time period can not be added to the cumulative audience of another time period. This is because some people included in one estimate will also be included in the second estimate and would therefore, be 'double-counted'.

Similarly, cumulative audience estimates for different stations may not be added together to provide a cumulative audience estimate for a two-station combination. The reported audience to any given station is likely to include a proportion of listeners on any other reported stations.

In brief, cumulative audiences across different demographic groups may be added together (providing those demographic groups do not overlap) but cumulative audience estimates for different sessions or for different stations may not be added together.

When buying or selling radio, is it better to use Averages or Cumes?
Both pieces of information can be vitally important in assessing alternative station buys.

Average audience allows a basic review of cost-effectiveness through the calculation of cost-per-thousand. However, average audience only reflects the total impact of a campaign without regard to audience duplication. ie the number of different people reached by the campaign.

If the prime campaign objective is to maximise reach, then other things being equal, cumulative audience estimates will reflect the preferred alternative. For example, assume two stations A and B have the same average audience figure, yet station A's cume is higher than station B's. A typical campaign schedule on station A is likely to reach more people (with a lower frequency) than the same schedule on station B. As average audience is the same on both stations, total impacts will be the same.

Cost Efficiency
Is the relation between a medium (or media-schedule's) audience and the cost of using that medium (or media schedule). "Cost per thousand" (CPM), "Cost per TARP" etc. are measures of cost efficiency.

Cost Per TARP or Cost Per Target Audience Rating Point
Is the advertising cost of reaching each 1% of potential for a specified 'target audience' with a particular media vehicle. The term is usually associated with TV. (see also "TARP").

Cost Per Thousand (C.P.M.)
Is the advertising cost of reaching 1,000 units of audience with a particular media vehicle. It is calculated by dividing advertising unit cost (at a specified cost level) by audience in thousands. As a measure of cost efficiency, C.P.M.'s are used to compare media vehicles. In print media, C.P.M. can also refer to cost per thousand circulation. (The 'M' in C.P.M. is the Roman Numeral for 1,000)

Coverage
At its simplest means the (geographic) extent of a medium within an area. "Coverage" is also used to describe the extent of a medium in reaching a group of people. The term is also used to describe the performance of the target audience having a chance to hear the commercial message.

Coverage Area
Refers to the geographic area claimed by a given television or radio station to be capable of receiving adequate reception. In some cases distinction is made based on signal strength, between "primary" and "secondary" coverage areas.

Day Part
Refers to a section of the day and reflects changing audience habits from breakfast to morning to afternoon to evening.

Demographics
Is a term used in media to describe audience classification by characteristics such as age, sex, etc. In media usage the term is synonymous with "audience composition" and "classification data"

Diary Method
Is the collection of media audience data through individual or household diaries. These diaries are designed to record the individual's or household's use of the medium in question for specific lengths on time. To ensure most accurate results, media diaries should be personally placed with respondents and personally collected. The major advantage of the diary method (in broadcast media) is that it can provide the demographic data required by all sections on the industry.

Effective Frequency
Describes the number of media exposures required to convey the advertising message. Its use is in both planning and evaluating campaigns with frequency expressed as a minimum or optimum requirement of say, 3+ exposures.

Awareness, Interest, Desire and Action

Exclusive Audience
Is the number, or proportion, of a given target audience that is reached only by a nominated media vehicle and not also by competitive media vehicles. Most commonly the term applies to broadcast media to illustrate the audience or reach of a specified (or stations) to the exclusion of other stations.

FPC
Full Page Colour.

Frequency Distribution
Shows how the cumulative audience (or reach) for a number of advertisements is made up in terms of the number and proportion of persons (or homes) who were reached once, twice, three times, etc. by a series of advertisements.

Gross Impacts
The total weight of people delivered by an advertising schedule without regard to audience duplication.*
Average Audience X Number of Spots = Gross Impact

* as defined by AC Nielsen McNair

Listeners
A listener is defined by AGB Australian Radio Surveys as someone who spends eight minutes or more of a specified quarter hour tuned to a particular radio station and who is within earshot of the spoken word.

Market Share
Is a company or brand's share of total industry sales volume. Also see "Share of Audience"

Media Mix
Means the combination of media (or media vehicles) used or suggested for a particular schedule or campaign.

Post Analysis
Refers to analysis activity in either the quantitative or qualitative sense undertaken after the appearance of specified advertisements. This may take the form, for example, of monitoring or assessing the "audience" actually achieved according to a current survey, or for example, in assessing advertising response, recall, etc.

RadioScope
Is a personal computer based program developed by AGB Australia which allows further analysis of Radio Audience data terms of Reach and Frequency including 'Multi-Week' formula based projections, Ebb and Flow, Multi Station Combination Cumulative audience, average audience and Station Shares.

Reach and Frequency
Refers to that form of analysis which, for a given advertising schedule, calculates the number (and proportion) of different people reached at least once by that schedule (cumulative audience), the total number of impacts made by that schedule and the average frequency with which the net audience was exposed to the commercial message of the schedule (Average Frequency).

Sample
A sample is the term used in survey sampling to describe the group (of people, homes, etc) selected for interviewing in the survey. The sample by definition has to be fully representative of the wider group (called "population" or "universe") from which it is drawn. See also "Cross Section".

Sessions (Cumes and Averages)
Refers to the day-parts Breakfast, Morning, Afternoon, Drive, Evening and Mid Dawn, in which audiences are tabulated either as averages or cumulatives within the nominated time periods.

Share of Audience
Is the percentage of the total radio listening audience in a given time period tuned to a particular station. "Share" is a station's rating expressed as a percentage.

S.C.CM
Single Column Centimetre.

Socio/Economic Data
Refer to those classifications of people in households relating to "class", income, occupation, etc

Target Audience
Is the term commonly used to describe groups in the community selected as being the most appropriate for a particular advertising campaign or schedule.

Time Spent Listening
Time spent listening data allows an advertiser to make a broad assessment of the number of announcements required to reach a certain proportion of a station's audience. Station management use time spent listening as an indicator of station loyalty among its listeners.

Print

Definitions supplied by A C Neilsen

Response curves. A graphic representation of the relationship between "frequency" (horizontal axis of chart) and "response" (vertical axis of chart) plotted for a specific product and conditions at a particular point in time. The resulting pattern is also called a "response function" (p. 94).

Rounding. See **Decimal.**

Seasonal rating adjustments. Broadcast rating modifications to reflect seasonal influences, such as weather, annual events, holidays, and media usage patterns (p. 97).

Share. The audience of a particular television program or time period expressed as a percent of the population viewing TV at that particular time (p. 80).

Target audience. That portion of the total audience defined to be the most likely purchasers of the product, that is, the total audience excluding waste (p. 69).

TRPs. See **Gross rating points.**

Wear out. The level of accumulated frequency or that point in time when incremental exposure to the commercial fails to contribute to the communication goals. Commercial wear out may even contribute to negative response in reaction to the advertising content, familiarity, or intensity (p. 94).

Weighting. A method of adjusting numbers to reflect additional considerations or value modifiers (p. 61).

TITLES OF INTEREST IN
PRINT AND BROADCAST MEDIA

ESSENTIALS OF MEDIA PLANNING, by Arnold M. Barban, Steven M. Cristol, and Frank J. Kopec

STRATEGIC MEDIA PLANNING, by Kent M. Lancaster and Helen E. Katz

MEDIA MATH, by Robert W. Hall

INTRODUCTION TO ADVERTISING MEDIA, by Jim Surmanek

MEDIA PLANNING, by Jim Surmanek

ADVERTISING MEDIA PLANNING, by Jack Sissors and Lincoln Bumba

ADVERTISING MEDIA SOURCEBOOK, by Arnold M. Barban, Donald W. Jugenheimer, and Peter B. Turk

THE FUTURE OF TELEVISION, by Marc Doyle

HOW TO PRODUCE EFFECTIVE TV COMMERCIALS, by Hooper White

HOW TO CREATE EFFECTIVE TV COMMERCIALS, by Huntley Baldwin

THE RADIO AND TELEVISION COMMERCIAL, by Albert C. Book, Norman D. Cary, and Stanley Tannenbaum

DICTIONARY OF BROADCAST COMMUNICATIONS, by Lincoln Diamant

CHILDREN'S TELEVISION, by Cy Schneider

FUNDAMENTALS OF COPY & LAYOUT, by Albert C. Book and C. Dennis Schick

CREATING AND DELIVERING WINNING ADVERTISING AND MARKETING PRESENTATIONS, by Sandra Moriarty and Tom Duncan

HOW TO WRITE A SUCCESSFUL ADVERTISING PLAN, by James W. Taylor

ADVERTISING COPYWRITING, by Philip Ward Burton

STRATEGIC ADVERTISING CAMPAIGNS, by Don E. Schultz

WRITING FOR THE MEDIA, by Sandra Pesmen

THE ADVERTISING PORTFOLIO, by Ann Marie Barry

PUBLIC RELATIONS IN THE MARKETING MIX, by Jordan Goldman

HANDBOOK FOR BUSINESS WRITING, by L. Sue Baugh, Maridell Fryar, and David A. Thomas

HANDBOOK FOR PUBLIC RELATIONS WRITING, by Thomas Bivins

HANDBOOK FOR MEMO WRITING, by L. Sue Baugh

HANDBOOK FOR PROOFREADING, by Laura Anderson

HANDBOOK FOR TECHNICAL WRITING, by James Shelton

UPI STYLEBOOK, by United Press International

FUNDAMENTALS OF SUCCESSFUL NEWSLETTERS, by Thomas Bivins

BUSINESS MAGAZINE PUBLISHING, by Sal Marino

THE PUBLICITY HANDBOOK, by David R. Yale

NTC'S MASS MEDIA DICTIONARY, by R. Terry Ellmore

NTC'S DICTIONARY OF ADVERTISING, by Jack Wiechmann

DICTIONARY OF BROADCAST COMMUNICATIONS, by Lincoln Diamant

HOW TO PRODUCE CREATIVE ADVERTISING, by Ann Keding and Thomas Bivins

HOW TO PRODUCE CREATIVE PUBLICATIONS, by Thomas Bivins and William E. Ryan

For further information or a current catalog, write:
NTC Business Books
a division of *NTC Publishing Group*
4255 West Touhy Avenue
Lincolnwood, Illinois 60646–1975